Developing Teen Leadership: A practical guide for youth group advisors, teachers and parents

by

Dan Appleman

Desaware Publishing
San Jose, California

First Edition

ISBN: 978-1-936754-00-7
Library of Congress Control Number: 2010943116

Printed in the United States of America.

www.TeenLeadershipBook.com

Contents

Introduction

Imagine a group of teenagers. They are self-confident, ambitious, responsible, able and eager to set goals and accomplish them. They treat each other well, supporting each other in times of need, and even when it isn't particularly needed. They have good moral values, and academic success is prized. And while they welcome and even seek out advice from trusted adults, they actually manage their group with virtually no adult supervision.

I doubt there is a youth counselor, advisor, teacher, scoutmaster, or youth minister who would not be thrilled to work with or help create a group like that. And it's hard to imagine a parent who would not wish their own son or daughter to be part of such a group, and have the opportunity to become a leader in such a group.

That such groups exist at all remarkable given the attitude much of our society has towards teens. Adults may say they want teens to become leaders, but their actions more often ask for obedience, passivity, and conformity. Teens are expected to respect adults, but are granted little respect in turn. They are much more likely to receive a lecture than an understanding and fair hearing.

Yet such groups exist, and in most cases you will find an adult, somewhere in the background, providing just a little bit of guidance.

This book is written for those adults.

They come with many titles, such as counselor, scoutmaster, youth minister, youth pastor, adult guide, advisor, youth advisor, and so forth (though throughout this book I use the term "advisor" to represent all of these roles). And they all have the same goal – to help young people to learn, to grow, to build friendships and to become confident leaders while in a safe environment.

Before writing this book, I looked for books on developing youth leaders – and there are a few. But they mostly seemed to be written by "experts" – psychologists and other specialists on adolescent development. And while they have plenty of jargon and analysis, they seemed to lack the down-to-earth practical knowledge that is needed by those who work in the trenches. If you are an expert, a psychologist, a social worker or therapist, I encourage you to read one of those books. Why, you can even write one of your own.

This book is for the counselors, advisors, teachers, scout-masters and parents who are not "experts". It contains real-world practical information and techniques that you can use every day to help teens become real leaders. You won't find psychological jargon or endless tracts on adolescent psychology. Instead, you'll find advice that works.

How do I know it works? Because I have spent over 20 years working with a group that comes as close as you could imagine to the kind I described at the start of this introduction. Every idea, hint and technique you'll read here is based on the real world experience of myself and others I've worked with. And I know they will work for you.

Note to teachers and parents

While this book has been written with an eye towards adults working with groups of teens, much of the material is directly relevant to teachers and parents as well. Towards the end of the book, you will find a chapter for teachers and one for parents that offer a perspective on how you can apply the ideas and techniques in this book and adapt them to your own situation.

Developing Teen Leadership:
A practical guide for
youth group advisors, teachers
and parents

Part I – Guiding Principles

Principles exist to help us figure out the right thing to do in situations that are new to us, and believe me – if you are working with teens, you will definitely experience situations that are new and unexpected. The guiding principles you find here will help you figure out what to say and what to do.

Many of the sections contain sample phrases that illustrate the principles in that section. These practice phrases should become part of your standard vocabulary when talking with teen leaders. Obviously, you'll want to put them in your own words. Whatever you do, don't try to put them in the teen's words. First, you probably don't know their words (the language changes that quickly[1]). Second, you are not a teen so don't try to sound like one - you'll be seen a fool if you do. Just be yourself.

---

[1] If you need help translating the latest teen phrases, check out http://www.urbandictionary.com. Be aware that it has content many would consider inappropriate (if not profane), and it is not always accurate.

1 - Anything they can do, they should do

If you want teens to learn leadership, you must let them lead.

That sounds rather obvious, doesn't it? Yet it's astonishing how many adults try to teach leadership by taking on the leadership role themselves and hoping that the teens will follow their example.

Now, it is true that setting an example is the most crucial part of being a leader. And it is true that as an adult, you should be a role model. But if you want the teens to become leaders, they have to learn to be role models and set the examples for each other.

So one of the most important principals of teaching youth leadership is to get out of the way and let them be leaders.

Or put another way: If there is a task that the teens are capable of doing, you must step back and let them do it. Even if they do not do it the way you would, or as well as you would. Even if it takes them longer than it should, or if they make mistakes along the way. Even if there is a risk of failure.

This is actually the hardest part of teaching leadership for most adults. The temptation to step in and "do it right" or "show them how" is incredibly powerful. Yet that is exactly what you must do.

Here are some phrases for you to practice:

- What are you going to do about it?
- It's your problem, not mine
- That's not my job. You're the leader, you handle it
- Let me know what you decide

If you want teens to learn leadership, you **must** let them lead.

2 - Don't try to get them to like you; earn their respect

As an adult working with teens, it's natural to want to be liked. Many adults, when starting to work with a group of teens, make an effort to be liked. This is almost always a mistake.

Your first priority when working with a group of teens must always be to earn their respect. The reason for this is simple: If you fail to earn their respect, they will not learn from you, and you will be wasting your time. If you do earn their respect, not only will they learn from you, they will actually end up liking you as well.

Of course, this raises an interesting question: How do you earn the respect of a group of teens?

First and foremost, recognize that you must **earn** their respect. You must prove worthy of it. You can't just expect it, you can't demand it, and you can't just insist on the trappings of respect (like insisting they call you "Sir" or "Ma'am"). You have to prove that you deserve to be respected, and be willing to work to prove it.

Recently an advisor asked me whether it shouldn't work both ways. Shouldn't the teens have to earn the advisors respect as well? I surprised him when I answered no. If you look at it as a two way street, you can quickly fall into a "who earns respect first" dilemma – each side saying, "Well, I'll earn your respect as long as you earn mine." As the adult in the relationship, it is your job to always strive to earn respect, regardless of what the teens do or say. That may not make sense at first, but here's the kicker: every teen wants to be respected by the adults that they respect. So if you can earn the teens respect, they will absolutely strive to earn yours as well. But the first move is always yours.

As far as earning respect goes, the rest is actually quite easy – follow the guiding principles in this book. The better you follow them, the more respect you will earn.

3 - Thou shalt not lie

Never, never, never lie to the teens you are working with. Every word you say to them must be what you truly mean and feel and believe to the very best of your ability. Sincerity is everything. I promise you that if you are insincere, dishonest, or manipulative they will see right through you and you will not be effective.

Here's a true story:

I was staffing a weekend camp retreat, and the coordinators were doing a simulation program that involved lying to the group – pretending that a disaster was happening so that the group would react, after which they would discuss and learn from the process.

One of the teen leaders from my group pulled me aside and asked me quietly if the disaster was actually happening or if it was a stunt. I had been instructed to keep the secret in order to preserve the integrity of the program. Nevertheless, I found it impossible for me to lie to him. Though I was much less experienced than I am now, I knew instinctively that lying to him, even for the sake of the program, would permanently damage our relationship and my ability to be an effective youth advisor. So I told him the truth, and then asked him not to give it away so that the program could continue. In doing so, not only was I able to maintain the trust we had developed, I was able to build on it – essentially telling him that I trusted his judgment on how to proceed.

Not lying does not mean you have to tell everything. There are many cases where you can, and should, simply refuse to answer. You can even explain why if you wish. But refusing to answer is a very different thing from lying, and teens can tell the difference.

Here are some phrases for you to practice:
- I'm sorry, I cannot answer that question because...
- I consider that a personal question, ask me something else...
- I may be wrong, but I truly believe that...[2]

---

[2] This one relates more to being accurate than honest. It is OK to let people know if you are not certain that what you are saying is true or accurate.

4 - Let them fail

It's hard enough for adults to sit back and let teens make decisions. It's even harder to sit back when you are sure that what they are about to do is a mistake or likely to fail. Yet this is what you must do.

Or as it was once put to me: it's OK to let them skin their knees, but not break their necks. If the decision they are about to make represents a real danger, then you should obviously step in. But if it's not dangerous, step back. It's ok to give a warning or offer advice – but if they aren't listening or interested in your opinion, don't push it.

We tend to learn from our mistakes; so obviously the best way to learn is to make plenty of mistakes. The teen years are a great time to do that, and giving them the freedom to make mistakes is one of the greatest gifts you have to offer. Let them know that you will offer advice, but they have the freedom to ignore it and do what they think is best.

After the mistake has been made is when your job really starts. Not with lectures or criticism (they're probably feeling bad enough anyway). Start with the question: "What would you have done differently?" Chances are they will have ideas of things they would change, and that opens the door to you offering your own suggestions of things they could have done differently. This way the failure turns into a learning experience and helps them become stronger leaders (which was your goal in the first place).

In fact, there are times where you might want to encourage failure. If a group is not failing at least part of the time, chances are they aren't ambitious enough. Or put another way – you can't fail at something if you don't try it. So if you aren't failing now and then, you probably aren't trying new things or pushing your limits.

There are some educators who feel that allowing kids to fail will harm their self-esteem; so they either step in to prevent failure, or make a big deal out of mediocre efforts. In fact, kids and teens benefit most when adults are giving accurate feedback on their performance. As most teens will tend to be overcritical when things go wrong, most of the time you'll find yourself emphasizing successes and where things went well.

Here are some phrases for you to practice:

- Are you sure you want to...?
- Have you considered...?
- It seems to me that ... might happen, but it's your decision.

And after failure:

- What would you have done differently?
- How do you feel about how things went?
- That was a problem, true – but look at the good things that happened.

5 - Limits

It is a well-known cliché that kids need limits and that they even want limits (for all that they may not admit it). And surely setting limits is part of your role. You'll want to make sure that activities are safe, and that your organization's rules are followed. This much is obvious.

Where most adults go wrong is not on the limit setting – it's with what happens up until the limits are reached. There is a strong tendency to try to control the activity regardless of where the limit is, and that control goes against the development of leadership among the teens.

The real challenge for you is allowing the teens to have complete control over the group as long as that limit is not reached. How do you do this? First, by figuring out what the limits are. Next, by communicating them to the group. Then, by making it clear both in word and deed that as long as they do not cross those limits, they have complete freedom to make their own choices and act on them. Finally, by strictly enforcing those limits that you have defined.

"Strictly enforcing" is not the same thing as mindlessly enforcing. After all, one of the reasons you are there is to help the teens figure out if a particular decision or activity lies within those limits. So you should be prepared to explain the reasoning behind your decisions, and you should be willing to listen to reasonable debate on those decisions. Why, if you listen hard enough they may actually persuade you that they are right – in which case I encourage you to compliment them on their reasoning and adjust the limit accordingly.

But there's a difference between reasoned argument and manipulation. If something is against the rules or does not meet with health and safety requirements, no pleading, guilt or emotional appeal should move you. They'll respect you more for standing up for what you believe in – nobody respects a pushover[3].

Here are some phrases for you to practice:

- I'm sorry, that is against the rules. I'll be glad to explain to you why that rule exists if you would like to know.
- If I were to let you do that, I would likely be fired, and rightly so.
- That won't work, but here's an alternative that might.
- If you do that, I will have no choice but to call your parents and ... I'd prefer that you not put me in that position.

---

[3] For an interesting illustration of this point, see "Insist on being treated like a person" in Chapter 54.

6 - Find ways to say yes

Teens and kids hear the word "no" all the time. It's no wonder many stop asking. The reality is that teens are generally capable of far more than they are ever expected or allowed to do. In fact, they are generally as intelligent and capable as adults – their lack of experience often serves as an advantage in that they do not know that something is impossible, and thus proceed to do it regardless.

Part of teaching leadership is to get teens to realize that they are capable of becoming leaders and accomplishing tasks. One of the best things you can do to encourage this is to, as much as possible, eliminate the word "no" from your vocabulary. Except for health and safety or rules issues (see Chapter 5); the answer should always be some variation of the word yes.

This sounds obvious and maybe even easy, but you will find it can be much harder than you expect. First, many times when the teens want to do something, it means more work for you – and it is human nature to want to avoid extra work (especially when, depending on the nature of your position, more work does not necessarily mean more pay). Second, in many cases when the teens come to you the question will be in the form of a challenge (such as "why can't we ...?"). When challenged, your natural reaction will often be to reject the request as a challenge to your authority. And once you've said no, you may feel trapped into continuing to say no even if you change your mind, because you may feel that to change your mind would undermine your authority in the future.

When teens come to you, even if it is in the form of a challenge, it's important to stop and think. Listen carefully to their argument and consider it. If the answer is no, put yourself in their position and see if you can think of a better argument, or a counter-proposal that might satisfy them.

Don't be afraid of changing your mind later – just be sure you have a good reason for changing your mind and express it. If you change your mind after you hear a good argument it will not undermine your authority – it will enhance it, because you'll be seen as someone who listens and respects other points of view.

Of course, changing your mind because people whine and annoy you into changing (not based on a good argument), will not only undermine your authority but will doom you to a constant stream of annoying whining. So don't do that.

Here are some phrases for you to practice:

- Interesting, how would you start tackling that project?
- What a great idea! I bet you could get others interested in helping you with it.
- You want to plan a trip to Japan? OK... let's sit down and figure out how that could be accomplished.
- You really can't wave a running chainsaw at new members during the initiation. But it seems to me you could get a good effect if you remove the cutting chain, keep the chainsaw off, stay at least six feet away and play a recording of a chainsaw. Would that be acceptable?[4]

---

[4] No, that is not a hypothetical question. It was a real question and that was my actual answer.

7 - Initiative and control

If you truly wish the teens you work with to become confident leaders, you will inevitably run into the following contradiction:

On one hand, you (as the adult) will always have some degree of responsibility for the group – particularly on issues relating to safety and rules, but also sometimes for other aspects of the program – depending on the type of program and the expectations of your particular organization.

At the same time, for the teens to actually lead, they have to have a degree of control over the program. The larger the degree of control, the more they will gain from the program in terms of developing leadership skills.

It's not fair or possible for you to have responsibility for things you have no control over. So you will find yourself in a delicate balance – trying to give the teens as much control as possible, while still maintaining enough control to fulfill your responsibilities.

One way you'll be tempted to handle this is to review all of their decisions – that way you'll at least know what is going on. However, this approach is flawed: it inevitably limits initiative, will be interpreted as a lack of confidence and trust, and establishes you as the person "in charge" of everything.

A better approach is to teach the teens what issues you do need to be informed about, and leave the rest to them (for example: health and safety or policy concerns). If they come to you regarding other issues, offer them advice but never permission. And when they make mistakes (which they will), address the mistakes without ever saying "why didn't you ask me first?"

The lesson you hope to teach is that it is often better to ask forgiveness than ask permission. There will be times where it will be very hard for you to let go enough to allow them to learn this lesson – but it is an essential part of leadership and initiative [5].

---

[5] The lesson, that is better to ask forgiveness than ask permission, is one you may wish to adopt in general in your role as advisor in the context of the organization you are working with. It will sometimes annoy your supervisors or management, but the organization and your group will almost always be better for it.

8 - Admit your hypocrisies

Kids and teens hate hypocrisy. Maybe it's a holdover from childhood when kids believe in the tooth fairy, in fairness, and that the good guys always win. This poses a challenge because unless you happen to be a practicing saint, you aren't perfect. We're all at least a little bit of a hypocrite.

But here's the thing – so are the teens. So your challenge is not to be perfect – they know you aren't perfect just as they know they aren't perfect. (Trust me, they spend much of their time stressing over how imperfect they are).

Your job is to set an example of how to deal with that hypocrisy, and the best example is to face it head on. Don't pretend to be something you are not. If they call you on a mistake, apologize and move on. Having the confidence to face your own errors and weaknesses sets a wonderful example and will give them the courage to do the same. And they will respect you infinitely more than they will if you try to fake it.

Here are some phrases for you to practice:

- I'm not nearly as good at ... as I should be.
- I know I should be doing ... It's one of my personal failures. Hopefully I'll do better.
- Don't stress, I'm not perfect either.

9 - Role modeling is everything

When you teach leadership, the single most important lesson to teach is the value of setting an example. Here's a situation that illustrates this:

One day the group was holding a discussion outdoors near a basketball court. One of the leaders of the group got up and started shooting baskets (which was quite annoying to the other leaders, and was definitely both a temptation and distraction to the rest of the group). I got up and pulled him over to talk. I explained to him that because he is a leader, when he does something, he is effectively giving permission for everyone else to do the same - even inviting them to join him. The question a leader must ask is "If everyone does what I want to do, would that be a good thing?" In this case, he realized that if everyone joined him the discussion would stop – which is definitely not what he intended. So he returned to the group – lesson learned (at least for the moment).

When teens think of leadership, they think of making speeches, giving orders and having everyone listen to and respect them. They don't necessarily think of being a role model – yet that is the single most important aspect of leadership.

This applies to adults as well.

Even though you are (hopefully) taking a back seat to let the teens take on the leadership roles, it is critically important that you act as a role model in the way you conduct yourself. Make no mistake, if you earn their respect, they will listen to you. They will remember what you say (even offhand comments that you won't remember saying). And your words and actions will have an impact.

What does this mean in practice?

- Don't forget the little things – the way you dress, shake hands, and relate to both teens and other adults.
- Remember the big things – punctuality, keeping your commitments and promises, the way you treat others. Be sure to treat the teens as you would want them to treat you – with respect.
- Do not tell them things about your life that are none of their business. Your two years being stoned while in college sets a bad example and should not be shared (besides, they'll figure out college on their own).
- Do tell them positive things that you've done in your life (but please, try to avoid the phrase "when I was a kid" as much as possible when doing so).
- What you post on social networking websites is forever – so either be careful what you post, or do not "friend" the teens or allow them access to any personal information.

10 - Apologize for your mistakes

You will make mistakes. Hopefully they won't be really big ones. Hopefully you'll catch them early. The secret to dealing with your mistakes is to apologize early and often. Apologize in person and in public.

Most teens are afraid to admit their mistakes. One reason is because doing so tends to be a sure way to get in trouble in our increasingly zero-tolerance society. Another is the fear that an apology makes you look weak, or that it will cause your friends to reject you.

In fact, apologizing (as any smart politician will tell you) is the first step towards redemption, and ironically tends to cause others to treat you with more respect. To apologize actually demonstrates confidence, and that is the example that you should set.

I make it a policy to apologize even for (if not especially for) mistakes that nobody else noticed. In doing so I not only demonstrate confidence and the ability to take responsibility for my mistakes, I demonstrate that I am striving to live up to my own standards – not just the judgment of others.

Here are some phrases for you to practice:

- I'm sorry, that was a screw up. Here's what I'm going to do to try to fix it. (or, what can I do to fix it?)
- I'd like to tell you about a mistake I made yesterday that you may not have noticed. Here's what I learned from it...
- I must cancel at the last minute. I apologize in advance if this causes a problem. Let me know if it does and I'll try to help resolve it.

;h expectations, but not perfection

...e generally capable of achieving far more than they believe. In truth, their biggest limit is lack of belief in what they can accomplish. You can help them develop that belief.

High expectations are one of the greatest gifts you can give. Setting expectations is NOT the same as telling them what to do (remember, we're talking leadership here). Setting expectations consists of expressing faith in the individual that he or she can meet those expectations. This can take the form of an explicit statement - expressing a belief that they can do something. It can also be expressed through a request to do something (not an order!).

While you set high expectations, you should not expect the teens to always or perfectly meet those expectations. When that happens it is important for you to reassure them that it's OK not to be perfect. It is also a good time to stress that you are not about to give up on them (unless you are, which can happen).

Here are some phrases for you to practice:

- Of course you can ....
- You clearly have the ability to .... ; the only question is what you choose to do.
- If you don't do it, it won't get done. It's up to you whether it is important enough to justify the effort.
- There's a problem ... and I believe you are the best person to tackle it. Would you be willing to give it a shot?
- I know you're not satisfied, but look at what you did accomplish! I'm certain next time you will do better, given what you learned today.

- Don't worry, just because you screwed up on this doesn't mean I hate you.[6]

Some phrases to avoid:

- I know you can do it – so do it NOW!
- I don't think you can do it – prove me wrong[7].

---

[6] Saying "I won't hate you" sounds a bit funny, doesn't it? That's because it is. But the hyperbole is intentional – it's taking the underlying fear of rejection, blowing it out of proportion, and laughing at it. When you're joking and laughing with someone you aren't rejecting them. Thus the humor is a way of lending support both in words and in action.

[7] Curiously enough, I was recently told by one of our graduates that I once had seemed a bit doubtful about his ambition to publish a record number of newsletters during his term. He then did so just to prove me wrong. I would still never take this approach, but it does illustrate an important point: You can't be certain how individuals will respond to something you do or say, and you may not know how they felt about it until years later.

12 - You really don't know best

As an adult there will be many times where the teens you work with will propose something that you think is absolutely nuts – that won't work, that won't be fun, or that will fail miserably. There will also be times where you will hear of some problem and you'll be absolutely convinced that you have exactly the right advice and know exactly what they should do.

And you'll be right – about half the time.

It is shocking the degree to which adults tend to be condescending towards kids and teens. There seems to be a natural assumption that just because you are older and more experienced, you know best. Teens are used to being treated that way, and all too often buy into it.

The truth is not so simple:

- Statistically speaking, unless you are particularly brilliant, about half of the teens you deal with will be smarter than you are. This means that despite their youth and lack of experience, their problem solving skills may well be better than yours.

- No matter what your experience, they have better knowledge of their own situation, likes and dislikes than you do.

What this means in practice is simple: don't assume that you know best. Take the time to ask questions and listen to their reasoning. Feel free to offer suggestions, but unless it is a matter of health and safety or a rules violation, let them make the call. You will be astonished to find that, more often than not, things work out just fine – and sometimes far better than you would ever expect.

13 - Wait – most problems solve themselves

One advantage adults have over teens is life experience. But what does life experience really mean? It means that there are large sets of problems where you have already experienced the alternatives, made the mistakes and learned from them (or watched others make the mistakes and learned from them). It means that you don't really have to think about the best approach for those problems – you already know the answer.

In other words – there are certain problems that you can solve quickly.

A teen might be smarter than you, but without the life experience, they have to puzzle out the solution. If it's a group, they might need to talk things over, discuss alternatives and argue for what they believe is the right choice. That takes time. *for parents and educators*

Lots and lots of time.

As someone who wants to teach leadership skills, one of the best things you can do when individuals or the entire group are dealing with an issue is sit back and wait. Don't rush in with advice. In fact, don't even express an opinion at first. With luck, you won't even need to act as a facilitator – just sit back and let them work things out. Most of the time, if you give them a chance they will come up with a solution that is at least "good enough". Sometimes they will come up with a better solution than the one you originally thought of.

So whenever your instincts tell you to step in (and it's not a true emergency) - stop. Wait. Be patient. Read a book. Take a nap. Give the teens the time they need to work things out for themselves.

14 - Be a back-seat driver

When you are teaching youth leadership, the last place you want to be is in front of the group leading.

Consider this example: What do you do if the teens trying to lead an activity are unable to get people to quiet down and listen to them?

Your gut reaction might be to stand up and tell everyone to "shut-up and listen". And while this might be the right approach for an extreme situation, in most cases it is the wrong choice — because it puts you in the role of a leader and invalidates the authority of the teen leaders.

A better approach is to pull one of the teen leaders aside and offer them some suggestions as to how to get the group to quiet down. Better yet, if the group consistently has a problem with cooperation, take the time to teach the group leaders techniques to accomplish this (I'll cover some of these techniques Chapter 39). Generally speaking, the only time you should be in front of the group in a leadership role is when you are teaching something (preferably leadership skills that they can use).

To become a leader, teens require both knowledge and experience. They need to learn about leadership and learn specific leadership skills. But they also have to practice those skills — that's where most youth leadership programs fail. They don't actually allow the teens to be leaders.

Your influence over the group (which will be significant once you earn their respect) should always be exercised in the background — mostly through discussions with the group's leaders. Listen to them, ask questions, and offer suggestions; but leave them with the actual decision and responsibility to execute the decision.

15 - Don't take it personally

We all tend to fall in love with our ideas. And when people dismiss our ideas, we have a natural tendency to feel like we're being dismissed. So what happens when you offer an idea or suggestion to a teen and they dismiss or ignore it?

Many adults get rather offended by this. After all, adults are older and wiser – what does that kid think he's doing ignoring such a great idea?

While you hope the teens will be polite about it, you actually want them to be willing to dismiss your ideas – that means they are making decisions. When this happens, don't take it personally. Dismissing your idea is NOT the same thing as dismissing you.

Things get trickier when they break a rule. When you've told someone to do something and they don't do it, or not to do something and they do it anyway, your first reaction may well be anger: "How dare that person ... !"

It is important to remember that in most cases when you are disobeyed their action has nothing to do with you personally. They are not acting to spite you. They are acting because of what they personally want or do not want to do.

So again, try not to take it personally. Instead, consider the circumstances. Was what you asked reasonable in the first place? If not, you may want to just ignore the whole situation, or have a friendly talk about it that does not include any consequences.

If the situation is one where some sort of consequences are necessary, try to find consequences that will actually have a positive impact – that will help them learn something from the experience. That will be hard to do if you are angry and personally offended by what they did.

Remember: you are working with teens, that means you must always be the adult in the relationship. You need to be calm and reasonable even if they are not.

16 - Talking back is good

I hate it when the teens I work with agree with everything I say. I love it when they disagree with me.

Most adults are the other way around – they want the teens they work with to worship every word they say. Any teen who dares to disagree or "mouth-off" is a smart-aleck, a troublemaker, or disrespectful. Those are generally the teens who get kicked out of the program or marginalized. It's tragic really, because they often make the very best leaders.

George Bernard Shaw said: "The reasonable man adapts himself to the world; the unreasonable one persists in trying to adapt the world to himself. Therefore all progress depends on the unreasonable man."

What are the characteristics of the "unreasonable man"? How about someone who disagrees, mouths-off, is a smart-aleck and a troublemaker?

Eshel Haritan said: "A leader is someone who drives change". Do you see where I'm going with this? If you kick out your troublemakers, you are probably removing your very best potential leaders!

You are really shooting for the teens to listen to your ideas and consider them on their own merits. You don't want the teens to reject your ideas out of hand just because they come from you – that's a sign that you haven't earned their respect yet (because they aren't actually thinking about the idea, only where it came from). Equally important, you do not want them to adopt your ideas blindly – that means that they are not yet acting as leaders, making their own decisions, and taking responsibility for them.

When a teen talks back or disagrees with you, that is your cue to listen. If the disagreement is polite and friendly, take the opportunity to compliment them on standing up for what they believe in. Then, invite them to turn their opinion or proposal into action.

If the disagreement is not polite or is angry, it is even more important to stay calm and listen. That's your cue to say: "I can see you feel very strongly about this. I'm ready to listen to what you have to say." In most cases the anger exists because their opinion has never been given credence by adults. So when you actually listen they will likely be thrown into a state of shock. Sad to say, I've had more than one occasion where a teen told me, after such a conversation, that I was the very first adult who actually listened to them.

Once you have listened, chances are they will have calmed down quite a bit. What next? You guessed it – compliment them on standing up for what they believe in and invite them to turn their opinion or proposal into action.

Here are some phrases for you to practice:

- Don't be afraid to disagree with me. I want to hear your opinion.
- One of the best ways to earn my respect is to disagree with me, especially if you do it intelligently and politely.
- Wow, what a great idea! I never thought of that!
- You may be right. So what are you going to do about it?
- I can see you feel very strongly about this. I'm ready to listen to what you have to say

You can read more on this topic in Chapter 48, "Bad kids and troubled teens".

17 - Plant seeds

Most of the time, when adults want a teen to do something or learn something, they want it right away. This inevitably leads to conflict, as the teen's schedule might not match the adult's – and the adult (naturally) feels that their schedule should take precedent. This kind of conflict most often happens with parents, but can happen to youth counselors and advisors as well.

View yourself as a farmer. Farmers plant seeds with every expectation that a harvestable crop will be months and even years away. Dropping hints, asking questions, sharing ideas and offhand comments can all serve as seeds when working with teens. Because you are not forcing them (lecturing, yelling, and so forth) they will hear those seeds of ideas and, believe it or not, they'll take root. Don't be surprised if you hear the exact same idea you hinted at presented as their own original idea a few months later. Maybe they'll credit you with the idea, maybe not – it doesn't matter. Because they've adopted it as their own, it will be much stronger than it could possibly be if you had insisted on it at the time.

Perhaps the single most powerful seed you can plant has to do with helping teens see their own potential. Younger teens will often look up to the older ones as role models, and be impressed with their skills and abilities – yet won't really be able to see themselves in that position (for all that it might be just a year or two away). In many cases they won't even try to tackle opportunities that exist because of sheer lack of confidence.

If you see the potential in someone, don't hesitate to tell them so. If you see a teen with potential (regardless of the nature of that potential), tell them what you see and why. Because they respect you, they will start seeing themselves in the same way and acting accordingly. I know it sounds impossible, but one positive comment to a 13-year old can start the process that will turn them into an outstanding, confident leader and role model a few years later.[8]

Here are some phrases for you to practice:

- I've been watching how you handled ... That's exactly the kind of approach that can help you become ...
- If you keep doing ... you'll be amazed at how much people will respect you in a year or two.
- You seem to be interested in taking on some more opportunities? Good, I can see you have what it takes to succeed. My job is to help you with that. So let me know if you need anything and I'll occasionally touch base to see how you're doing.
- I've been doing this for a while and have gotten pretty good at spotting potential leaders. I can see that you're one of them. Are you interested?

Notice something about these phrases? Not one of them pushes or really encourages the teen to do anything. Not one of them has an immediate call to action. The first two are simply observations. They subtly talk about potential and the benefits of becoming a leader. The last two express your faith in them and offer help, but both are qualified by a question – making it clear that the decision of how to proceed lies with them. That's why these phrases are seeds – they are small

---

[8] I can't overstate this enough. Even a brief conversation can change someone's life. I've had those conversations and it's almost scary to realize how impactful they can be. That's why it's so important that even your casual conversations be positive.

statements with no thought of immediate results. Some may not grow at all, but they do have great potential.

You are not a kid.

I know that at times you may act like one, a
fun. For example: when our group goes out to ~~l__ ~~ laser tag,
it's not unusual for me to not only participate, but prove to
them that I still have the ability (on occasion) to thoroughly
thrash most of them.

Nevertheless, you are not a kid. (If you're a teen counselor
working with younger kids, this applies to you as well.)

What does this mean in practice?

It means that you walk a fine line. You're their friend in
the sense that you can and should act in their best interest
and be there to support and listen to them. But you're not
their friend in that you are not their peer and generally
should not be hanging out with them socially outside of the
context of the organization you are involved in.

You're a teacher in the sense of teaching skills and helping
them to develop as leaders, but you're not their teacher in the
sense of grading them, judging them, and having authority
over them. (Remember – your authority should be limited to
health and safety and rules violation – beyond that the teens
should carry as much authority as they are able and willing
to handle.)

By and large, your personal life is none of their business.
Personal questions should be dismissed politely but firmly.
Moreover, this goes both ways. Their personal life is none of
your business unless they volunteer and want to discuss it.
Your professional or public life, however, can be shared –
and often should be as it is part of you being a role model.

Keep an eye on your online life as well. If you are going to be working with kids or teens, you really don't want your personal blog or social network profile pages to include the gruesome details and pictures of your latest drunken wild party. People get fired over that kind of thing.

Your organization will have rules and policies relating to how you should conduct yourself with the teens, and how the teens should conduct themselves. Most of them will make a lot of sense. Occasionally you will run into one that seems really stupid – if so, be sure you understand the reasoning behind it (whoever is in charge should be able to explain it to you). If you still think it's stupid, be sure you understand the risk you are taking if you choose to ignore it.[9]

Here are some phrases for you to practice:
- I won't answer that question. It's not appropriate and I would never ask it of you either.
- Thanks for the invitation, but I'm not available. I'll see you at the next event.
- I can see where you disagree with that rule, but if it's OK with you, I'd like to explain how that rule actually helps you and the group.

---

[9] It may seem odd that I don't simply say "follow all the rules." The problem is that we're dealing with real organizations. Which means some of the people who make the rules are idiots, and some of the rules may sound good in theory but simply don't work in real life. Some of the rules can actually reduce the safety of the teens in the program or actively hurt them (some of the zero-tolerance rules fall in that category). Sometimes rules are imposed from a national organization that are unsuitable for your community or violate local law or community standards. Some rules are so vague or poorly written that nobody can understand them. So it's easy to say "follow all the rules", but the reality is never that simple.

- I know that rule is stupid, but I really have no choice but to enforce it. I could get in big trouble if I did, as could you.

There is another reason to keep your personal life private – it will make you more effective as an advisor. Consider the "innocent" question: "Do you ever drink?" How do you answer this?

- You could say: "Yes, I occasionally have a beer with friend or cup of wine with dinner" – thus being a role model of responsible drinking as an adult.
- You could say: "No, I don't really need alcohol to have a good time" – thus being a role model of sobriety.

But both of these answers have a downside in that they potentially reduce the number of teens who will be willing to discuss this issue with you. If you give the first answer, teens who believe in sobriety (or children of alcoholics) may not trust your opinion – you've become a drinker in their eyes. And if you give the second answer, teens who drink may not trust your opinion, figuring you'll be judgmental or won't understand their point of view.

But if you answer: "Sorry, that's a personal question; but here are some things I know about alcohol use..." you've left things vague and open, and haven't given anyone a reason not to discuss this subject with you.

19 - Being there

Often the best thing you can do at a youth group event is absolutely nothing. Just showing up matters.

When you show up, you are demonstrating that you believe the group and what the teens are doing is important. Your time is valuable (and it's OK to say so now and then). But being there is a worthwhile use of your time (and it's OK to say that as well).

Some people talk about "quality time". The problem with the idea of quality time is that you have no idea when that time will be. The only way to have those quality time moments is to spend plenty of "quantity time" – to be around when those golden moments happen when you can really have an impact.

Just being there helps group leaders to do the right thing. I remember overhearing one conversation in which a chapter leader explained that the group could not do something because I was watching. In fact, I would absolutely have let them do it – the leaders were using me as an excuse, and that was just fine. Just having an adult present makes a huge difference in moderating group behavior – even if you say nothing.

While you are there, don't feel you have to be constantly doing something. It's not unusual for me to bring a laptop and work while at events, or read a book or magazine, or even take a nap. With the youth in charge and running things, and responsible enough to call me if I'm needed, I have a great deal of flexibility as to how much attention I need to pay to what is going on. It may seem odd, but when a group is very active (the one I work with has one or two events every week), this flexibility is essential to avoiding burnout over the long term. At some events I am very engaged and pay close attention; at others I am somewhat detached. It depends on various factors including the type of the event. But either way, I'm present (or my co-advisor or other responsible adult is present), and that matters.

Kathleen Dollard expressed the importance of being present to me thus: "Teen empowerment is not the same thing as teen abandonment". The vast majority of teens want support from adults, and it really is an honor to be welcomed as an advisor for a youth group.[10]

---

[10] When I was first asked to become a group advisor (by the teens themselves), I was astonished that they actually wanted an adult around and considered it a huge compliment. I have never lost that feeling.

20 - Consistency

Who wants to be totally predictable?

Answer: you do.

I talked earlier about the importance of setting limits. It is equally important that those limits be consistent. It's a good thing for teens to know where you stand, and that a limit you establish today will be in place tomorrow.

It is important for them to be able to count on you – to return phone calls, to arrive on time, to keep your promises. All of this is part of being a role model. All of this contributes to earning respect.

You should strive to be the most consistent and predictable person your teens know.

That said...

Sometimes, when it does not involve something fundamental relating to your role, you should feel free to shake things up.

For example: every now and then, I have to chaperone a community dance (not, I confess, my favorite thing). Some years back I teamed up with another regional advisor and we showed up to a couple of dances in costume: once dressed in our finest 18th century formals, once as a Vulcan and Bajoran in full Starfleet uniform. Doing so did not compromise our ability to do our jobs, nor did it in any way take away from the program. What it did accomplish was to shake up people's perceptions. We set an example of adults having fun, of taking chances, and of not worrying about what others think.

So yes, strive to be consistent, reliable and predictable.

But don't overdo it.

21 - Who owns the group?

What makes a good leader? That's a question I'll answer in more depth Chapter 39. For now, let's focus on what is perhaps the single most important characteristic of a good leader: someone who puts the needs of the group equal to or ahead of their own interests.

Or put another way: a good leader cares about the group and its members.

This is somewhat obvious when you think about it. After all, if you don't care about what the group is doing, and don't care about the other members, why on earth would you want to lead? You might as well sit back and just enjoy whatever happens.

For someone to want to lead, the following must be true:

- A leader cares about the group and the people being led and wants to influence the direction of the group.
- A leader believes they can have an impact. There is no such thing as a powerless leader.

A leader must feel responsible. A leader must have authority. The two go hand in hand.

There are many so-called teen leadership programs where neither applies. The classic examples are some school student governments, where the class officers are in it for reasons of popularity (and sometimes don't actually care about anything beyond how it looks on their college application), and where they have no real authority to make decisions or instigate changes (which is part of why they don't care – what's the point of caring if you can't make a difference?).

For teen leadership to happen, the teens must have real responsibility and must carry real authority. That's not to say unlimited responsibility and authority – but it must be significant enough to matter. One term people use to describe this is "ownership".

Who owns the group?

The teens should own the group.

Parents are often particularly concerned with how their children's actions reflect on them as parents. If you yourself view the group as belonging to the teens and not you – if you see yourself as an advisor and not an owner of the group – you'll be able to avoid that trap and stay clear-headed and objective regardless of what is happening (which is part of not taking things personally – see Chapter 15). More important, if you aren't taking ownership of the group, it becomes much more likely that the teens will. And once they do, they will care more about the group and see themselves (correctly) as having control over the destiny of the group. In other words: they will truly become leaders.

22 - Trust

Trust works in two directions.

That you should be trustworthy goes without saying. The teens in the group should trust you:

- To be honest
- To be consistent
- To listen patiently
- To not overreact to what you might hear
- To be slow to anger
- To keep your promises

And so on.

If you prove yourself trustworthy and reliable, you will inevitably earn their respect and be more effective in your role.

When it comes to trusting the teens, things are a bit trickier. After all, they will make mistakes and will sometimes fail to live up to the trust they are given.

Yet trust them you must. The question is exactly when and how to do this?

There are a number of techniques you can use:

- **Express trust**. When you trust the teens to do something or conduct themselves in a certain way, don't assume they can read your mind or magically figure out that you trust them. Be explicit. Point out that you are trusting them with something, but not in an accusatory manner. Don't say, "I'm trusting you with this, don't let me down!" Instead express your confidence in them in a matter of fact manner. For example, "I can do ... because I'm trusting you with ... If you run into any problems or questions, let me know. I know you'll do fine".

- **Set them up for success**. I discussed the earlier principle that anything the teens can do they should do (see Chapter 1). The flip side is that you should not trust them to do something that is clearly beyond their ability. Doing so is setting them up for failure. Here's an example: At one winter convention, a youth leader had a serious program planned and was trusting the rest of the group to take it seriously. During the program it started snowing outside. This may not sound like a big deal, but this was in a part of California where it almost never snows. The teens first became restless, and then left in a mass exodus to play in the snow. The teen leader was upset that they did not live up to his trust in them. I had to explain to him that it was not personal, nor was it really a failure in trust. It would have taken chains and handcuffs to keep those teens quietly inside under the circumstances.

  As much as possible, you want to trust the teens with things that they are able and likely to succeed at. If the challenge is one they are likely to fail at due to inability, lack of skill, or overwhelming temptation, don't rely on trust alone. Address the issue directly, provide help or support, change the rules, or otherwise do what is necessary so that they can get through the situation without breaking trust.

- **Trust, but verify**. If the teens tell you they've done something or made certain arrangements, don't be afraid to quietly verify this in the background. You don't have to tell them you have done so, but you can if you wish. If you don't and they catch you at it, don't get defensive. In either case, the explanation is simple: "I trust you, but I'm required to verify things as part of my job." In other words – blame the boss or organization's policy. This is not dishonest – I'll bet that if you ask your supervisor about your organization's policies, you will find that you are expected to supervise and verify many of their actions. For example: our youth group publishes a newsletter. I trust them to not put anything inappropriate in the newsletter, and 99% of the time that trust has been well placed. It is also organization policy that I review the newsletter. So what happens? Whenever they want to do a newsletter, they run it by me first. I do a quick review and pass it back – there's rarely an issue.

If they are planning a trip and make a reservation, I am expected to review it. Again, I trust their judgment, and there is rarely a problem.

If the outcome is not critical, don't bother verifying. If things go well, that's great. If they don't, the teens will learn a valuable lesson and have the opportunity of dealing with the resulting consequences – another great learning experience.

- **Tolerate failure**, then reestablish trust. Sometimes you will trust and that trust will be betrayed. When this happens, don't take it personally (remember Chapter 15!) When they've broken trust they know it. Address the issue in an open and straightforward manner, then determine what needs to happen for you to trust them again.

  You'll sometimes hear parents say "I see you can't be trusted, it will be some time before I trust you again." While true, this is not sufficient. You want to establish specific actions they can take to regain your trust. For example: our group once planned a camping trip that, while successful in the end, had a number of issues come up where I had been misled or they had failed to live up to commitments they had made. I was quite upset at the time, but took no immediate action as there were no safety issues involved.

After the trip, I met with the group and laid out the situation and problem areas. As they came to understand the problem, they realized that they had, in fact, violated the trust I had placed in them. But I did not leave it at that. I went on to explain that under the circumstances I would have a problem approving a major program or event, but that I would do so for anyone who attended a training session on event planning which I would run. Soon after, we held the training session that not only taught specific skills, but examined the issues from the camping trip and discussed how they could have been avoided. As far as I was concerned, that was sufficient to reestablish trust.

23 - Remember the positive

It is human nature to focus on problems. I don't know why that is, but we all have a tendency to focus on what is wrong. And when it comes to teens, most adults are quick to criticize and slow to compliment.

That makes it all the more important that you remember to stay positive. Compliments for a job well done (or even a particularly insightful statement) are always in order. Be particularly aware of opportunities to point out behavior that isn't always noticed or acknowledged. For example – if you see someone help someone else without being asked, you might publicly point that out as an example of outstanding conduct. Making a bit of a fuss over decent behavior will help encourage more decent behavior.

But remember, for your compliments to carry weight they must reflect actions that are truly worthy of acknowledgement. If you can't say something nice, then definitely remain silent – don't make something up, or exaggerate the importance of something for the sake of being able to say something positive.

24 - Turf and communication

Having reached over 20 years as a youth advisor, I've been around long enough to see the impact that technology has had on youth groups and my own role. Nowhere is this more apparent than when it comes to communication.

When I started, most communication took place during meetings or by phone (corded at home). Those days are long gone. Now most group business is done over instant message, email, cell phones (usually text messages), and social networking sites.

These new technologies have helped me become considerably more effective. In the old days when a problem came up in the group, it could take days to reach all those involved, figure out what was happening and facilitate a solution. Today, I can often reach all of the participants simultaneously via instant message or chat, holding multiple conversations at once. I can invite the parties into a chat room to discuss the issue, or can advise individuals to set up their own private conversations to talk over the problem. As a result, problems that once took days to address (and sometimes got worse due to the delay) can now be addressed and resolved in minutes, before they are blown out of proportion.

Different organizations have different policies regarding online communication, so you should find out what your organization's rules are. However, despite a certain degree of paranoia that some folks have (particularly those who are ignorant of or have not adopted the latest technology), online communication is actually safer for all concerned. While the media plays up incidents such as the Mark Foley scandal (the congressman who sent inappropriate instant messages to a congressional page), the unmentioned flip side was equally important: had Foley's messages **not** been inappropriate, the logged messages would have defended him (in a way that an unrecorded phone conversation would not). The lesson for you? Obviously, all online communication (and other communication) should be appropriate. Some youth advisors keep logs or copies of some or all instant message conversations as well.

There is a reason why I am stressing the importance of online communication that goes beyond the fact that it is more effective. To understand this importance, consider the difference in the way communication works in an adult-led vs. a youth-lead organization.

The following figure illustrates the structure of a typical adult led organization:

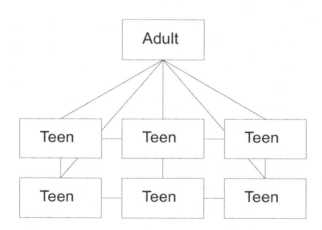

As you can see, the primary lines of communication are between the adult and the teens. While some of the teens might be in leadership roles, information tends to flow through the adult. A key part of leadership is controlling the information flow, so in an adult run organization not only is the adult aware of what is going on in the group, he or she is controlling and filtering the information. This also implies control over the means of communication, so the adult inevitably requires that the teens communicate on the adult's turf using the adult's preferred means of communication.

A youth led group looks very different, as you can see in the following figure:

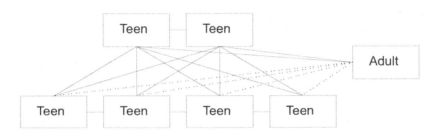

When the youth are leading, they have control over the communication flow. The teen leaders are communicating with each other and with everyone in the group. The adult's primary communication is with the teen leaders. As you can see, the adult's role is somewhat to the side – a true advisory role rather than a controlling role. The adult does have communication with all members of the group, but it is more casual and informational (as indicating by the dotted line) – more likely to be in the form of personal advice to members than group related issues. The idea is that if you, as the adult advisor, discover any issues or concerns while communicating with members, you can discuss those issues with the teen leaders and have them address the issues with the members, rather than doing so yourself.

This can be a difficult structure for an adult advisor to adjust to. For one thing you must accustom yourself to not knowing everything that is going on in the group. Since you are no longer controlling communication, some of the discussion and decision making will go on without you (this is a good thing). Your focus becomes working to be aware of what is going on rather than controlling what is going on. And yes, it does require quite a bit of trust in the teen leaders to adopt this kind of structure (see Chapter 22 on trust), but I guarantee you that it is worth it. It is the kind of structure that truly builds leadership skills.

In this kind of organization structure, the teens control the communication and thus also control the means of communication. In order to be effective you must visit their turf and use the same tools that they use. That means instant message, email, message boards, social networking sites, text messages, or whatever means of communication tomorrow's technology will bring.

Part II - Techniques

In Part I of this book you learned the guiding principles that you'll need to earn respect and help the teens you work with develop into strong and confident leaders. Even though I called them guiding principles, I think you'll agree that they were actually very practical. After all, a principle is not worth much if you do not understand how to put it to use.

This part of the book will focus on specific techniques. Every leader has a "bag of tricks" – techniques and methods that we use every day to accomplish our goals. In the chapters that follow, you will learn the most important of these techniques. They have two things in common:

First, they all work.

But just as important, every one of these techniques can be used by the teen leaders themselves within their own group! In other words, not only should you learn and use these techniques, I strongly encourage you to teach them to the teens you are working with. They'll work just as well for them; and trust me, in most cases, you'll be the first person to teach them these skills. As they try these techniques and use them, you will gain even more respect and credibility as an advisor – and become that much more effective.

25 - Positive-Negative-Positive

Confrontation is an inevitable part of both counseling and leadership. Confrontations can take many forms. It might involve pointing out a personal weakness or area where skills need to be improved. It might be criticism about a job not being done or promise not being kept. It might be a more serious issue, such as confronting someone about dangerous or illegal conduct.

In any case, the best way to handle the confrontation is as follows:

1. Open with a positive comment or compliment. It is a rare individual for whom you cannot find something positive to say.
2. Address the issue or behavior – not the person.
3. End on a positive note.

Consider this poor example addressing someone who did not do something that was promised:

"I just found out that you did not arrange for chairs for the event. I don't know how you could be so irresponsible. Now somebody else is going to have to scramble to arrange for enough chairs. Not only does this make you look bad now, but people won't trust you next time when you make a promise."

I guarantee you that whatever the reason was for the failure, that teen is going to feel awful – possibly to the point of quitting the group. Certainly, he or she will be less likely to take on responsibility and leadership roles going forward.

Using the positive-negative-positive approach, the confrontation might go like this:

"You're a responsible and respected member of the group who has great leadership potential. I know you're going to be very successful, but right now it seems we have an issue in terms of getting chairs for the event, which was your responsibility. Later we'll get together and find out how this happened, but right now I'd like to hear your ideas on how we can address the issue, and what kind of help you need so that we can solve this problem as a group. I'm sure when the group sees you taking responsibility now, it will go a long way to preventing your reputation in the group from being harmed. And once we have a chance to figure out what went wrong, we'll be able to figure out a way or I'll teach you the skills, so this kind of thing won't happen in the future – and you'll become an even stronger leader going forward."

This approach is vastly more effective. The opening positive statement not only expresses respect but establishes you as being on their side. The criticism is specific to the conduct and not personal. It also offers a specific and positive solution or action for how to proceed. It even attempts to take a bad situation and, if not turn it into a positive, at least make it a learning experience. It closes with an expression of faith and confidence along with a specific offer of help, again confirming that you are on their side.

There is another reason why this approach works:

When someone criticizes you (a form of attack), the first and natural response is to become defensive. In the case of teens, this often means not listening. Most parents have experienced this, whether in the form of a dazed look, increased music or video game volume, or a slammed door. So criticism alone simply does not work, as communication shuts down early in the process.

The positive-negative-positive approach prevents this from happening. What is your first reaction when someone compliments you? *You want to hear more!* After all, anyone who compliments you must be a very wise individual indeed. The positive opening not only enables communication, it establishes you as someone whose opinion is important.

By the time you sneak in the criticism, they are already listening. As long as the criticism is factual and addresses the behavior, there's a good chance they will keep listening. In this example, "we have a problem" is sufficient. The teen already knows that it was their responsibility and failure – you don't need to rub it in.

Phrases like "you are irresponsible" are personal attacks and will tend to close off communication. If you must use the word irresponsible, focus on the behavior: "not ordering the chairs was irresponsible" is very different from "you are irresponsible". See the difference?

Closing the confrontation on a positive note helps ensure that your relationship remains solid for next time. The teen will know that even if there is a problem (and there likely will be), that you are ultimately on their side and will be there to help them resolve the situation.

Teen leaders should be taught to use this technique as well. One of the best ways to teach this is through practice and role-playing: come up with a list of situations and challenge them to role-play the right and wrong way to handle the confrontation. Be sure to explain why this technique works.

Positive-Negative-Positive is by far the most effective way to handle a confrontation and is a critical leadership skill.

26 - Sticks and stones

In the last chapter, you learned the overall approach of sandwiching criticism between two compliments. I also introduced the idea of criticizing the behavior and not the person. In this chapter, we'll build on that concept.

There's an old rhyme you may have heard as a kid: "Sticks and stones can break my bones but words can never hurt me." Every kid knows that's nonsense, and I think by and large our society has come around to the idea that words can, in fact, hurt. They can help as well. So your choice of words is extraordinarily important.

Let's start by building on what you've already learned.

Criticize the behavior, not the person

Sometimes the difference between these is subtle, but it really does make a difference.

"That was a stupid thing to do" is better than "You're stupid."

"Most people would see that as a mean thing to do" is better than "You're a mean person."

"You did not do that well" is better than "You are incompetent."

Why is labeling a person bad? First, because it is destructive – it really can harm a person's self-esteem. Second, because in most cases the label does not correspond to the individual's own self-image. So as soon as you use a negative label, something they know is incorrect, they stop listening to everything else you have to say – and communication stops.

If you apply the label to the action, you can continue to talk about the action instead of the person. What was wrong with that action? How could the job have been done better? Why would someone see that as mean? By focusing on the mistake rather than the person, you preserve the possibility of helping the individual learn from their mistake.

Note that while applying negative labels to a person is bad, the reverse is not true. It is perfectly fine to apply positive labels to someone who does something well. In fact, the best strategy is to use both approaches simultaneously.

"That was a brilliant thing to do – you must be pretty smart!"

"I can tell you are a responsible and conscientious leader based on the fine job you did."

"That was a very kind thing you did. It's so nice to work with good people like you."

See how you can compliment both the individual and the action? Complimenting the individual helps build their confidence and self-esteem. Pointing out the action shows that you are not just being nice but are basing your evaluation on hard evidence.

When teaching this technique to teens, you might want to let them brainstorm ways to express both criticism and compliments using their own language (don't expect the teens to phrase things the way I did here[11]).

Ask, don't tell

When confronting someone, leading questions are often more effective than statements.

---

[11] Why don't I use samples of the teen's language here? Because it changes too quickly and varies by location. For example: at this moment if someone said, "Whoa, that's so sick" they would be extending a compliment, not noticing signs of a fatal illness.

"Could you have handled that situation better?" is preferable to "You handled that situation poorly."

"What would you have done differently?" is better than "Here's what you did wrong."

The questions are unequivocally critical, and thus should be the negative part of the positive-negative-positive conversation. It is obvious from the first question that the situation was handled poorly and from the second that things could have been done differently. But by asking a question, you accomplish two goals:

- You reduce the level of defensiveness. A statement is not only a stronger attack; it is essentially the opening salvo of a lecture, not a conversation. In a lecture, the speaker is active and the audience is passive – so it's very easy for the audience to stop listening.
- A question begs response. It asks the other person to actually think about the situation and respond. It initiates a conversation rather than a lecture. You dramatically increase the chances that the other person will actually learn something from the experience.

This technique is one of the harder ones to teach. For one thing, it's too easy to fall into the trap of using questions that aren't really questions at all. For example: "How could you do such a thing?", "What kind of idiot are you?" and "What were you thinking?", all of which are accusations, not questions. You might mention this approach as part of a leadership training program, but I would encourage emphasizing it only to your more advanced or experienced leaders.

I Statements

Frequently the most effective way to confront someone is to bring the focus to yourself by using an "I" statement: one that begins "I believe", "I think", "I saw" and so on.

Consider the following two statements:

"What you said was extremely offensive."

"I was offended by what you said."

The second is much more effective. Why? Because the first statement is subject to debate. The person you are confronting can argue that the statement was not, in fact, offensive at all. Next thing you know, you can find yourself in a debate about the statement itself rather than the decision to use it.

The second approach effectively prevents that debate. What is someone going to say – that you weren't offended? The person confronted might try to debate whether you should have been offended or not, but the fact that the statement was offensive to at least one person (you) becomes established fact due to the use of the "I" statement – only you can speak for yourself.

I can't stress how important this technique is. It is definitely one that you should teach your teen leaders, and one that lends itself well to role-playing.

By the way, if you look back at many of the sample phrases in this book you will find that a significant number, even a majority of them, are "I" statements.

27 - The power of indirection

When you are offering advice, never underestimate the power of asking a question or dropping a hint instead of speaking directly.

Consider, if you will, a phrase I've already used:

"When teaching this technique to teens, you *might want to let* them brainstorm ways to express both criticism and compliments using their own language."

Why didn't I say:

"When teaching this technique to teens, you *should have* them brainstorm ways to express both criticism and compliments using their own language."

After all, they say the same thing, don't they?

Yes and no. The latter approach is a more authoritative approach (and you will find there are many places in this book where I do use authoritative language – words like "should" and "must"). However, this approach does not encourage independent thought or build leadership.

By using the phrase "might want to", I am rejecting the authoritative role and taking on the role of a trusted and respected advisor who is sharing an idea or opinion. The suggestion is a gentle one – you know that I'll be perfectly fine with whatever you do and our relationship will not suffer whether you follow my suggestion or not. Moreover, by using the word "might" I imply that you might want to do something else – essentially inviting you to build on this idea or come up with your own.

Here are some additional examples:

"Have you considered trying..." instead of "You should try..."

"Here's a wild thought..." instead of "I have a great idea..."

"Feel free to ignore this, but I was wondering if you considered..." instead of "You must consider this..."

This particular technique is much more important for you, as the adult advisor, than for the youth leaders. Except for safety or rules issues, the subtle and indirect approach should be your primary approach (leaving the teen leaders to use the stronger more direct approach).

Nevertheless, it is important to teach this technique to the teens. It works best when they have delegated responsibilities to other teens and wish to offer advice or feedback without coming across as threatening or being seen as trying to take over.

28 - Don't be the boss

When people think about leadership, they often think of authority. It is easy to confuse the two. While exercising authority is a leadership skill, real leadership does not consist of telling people what to do. **Leadership consists of bringing people together to share a common vision of what they want to do.**

What is, after all, a community? A community is a group of individuals who share common values, common interests, and a common vision. Youth groups are almost all communities, whose effectiveness and closeness is largely determined by those commonalities.

A group leader is someone who has the ability to express that vision and translate it into action, or motivate the group to undertake an action by persuading them to change their shared vision.

For example: an authoritarian might get a group to help out at a local homeless shelter as follows:

"We're going to help out at a shelter. You, you and you – call the shelter, set up a date, and find out what they need. You – find out what they need and buy the supplies. You – make sure you get calls out to everyone in the group with the date and tell them they have to show up".

This approach is that of a "boss" and while it can be effective, it represents very poor leadership. Why? Because while people will participate, that participation will usually be less than enthusiastic. The members of the group will tend to wait for instructions rather than take initiative. And the boss will spend all their time running around, stressing out, and telling people what to do.

A leader might take this approach:

"Our group has a long tradition of helping the community. Homelessness is one of the biggest problems in our community and we can make a difference. We have the opportunity to help out at a local shelter and I'd like to hear your ideas about what we can do there. We'll come up with a plan and then I'll be looking for committee leaders to take responsibility for the specific tasks we decide on."

This leader starts out by defining a positive vision for the group. Next he or she lays out a plan of action. The plan is one that invites participation and challenges other teens to themselves take on leadership roles in the project.

With this kind of leader, members are more likely to be inspired and motivated. More important, they will be ready to take responsibility and initiative. Instead of worrying about every detail, the leader can focus on monitoring and coordinating the effort of others. The overall event is much more likely to be successful and rewarding for all.

As the adult, you should avoid telling the teens what to do unless a health and safety or rules issue is involved. But you can encourage and inspire them by helping to reinforce the vision and the values of the group. I often say that a good advisor acts, in part, as a mirror to the group – listening to what they wish to accomplish and then restating it in different words. The adult perspective that you can offer is a form of indirect leadership – one in which you can both reinforce good values and strengthen the teens in their own efforts to develop leadership skills.

Teaching teen leaders the difference between a leader and a boss will be an ongoing task. This is another case where role-playing different scenarios can be a useful teaching technique.

29 - Listening

I've heard it said that the sound most human beings love most is the sound of their own voice. Certainly, I've met many individuals who are much better at talking than listening. And this makes sense in a way. After all, we are each the center of our own little universe, and as the most important person in that universe; it is natural that our own thoughts and words are most important. Or as some put it, people often talk to themselves so that they can have someone intelligent to talk to.

This applies to teens as well, though in many cases they are more likely to talk to other teens than to adults. But the fact that many teens are unwilling to talk to adults is not all, or even mostly, their fault. The truth is that most adults are just terrible at listening (both to each other, and to teens and kids). So if you want to have the slightest hope of being heard, your first step is to learn how to listen effectively.

Active listening

When we think of two people talking, we tend to think of the speaker as the one taking action, while the listener is passive. No wonder verbal communication so often results in misunderstandings. Good listening takes work. It takes attention. It's not just a matter of focusing on what is being said, it is also a matter of giving feedback to the speaker that yes, you really are listening. One of the best ways to do this is called "active listening".

Active listening consists of not just listening, but of also giving feedback to the speaker. Some obvious ways of doing this are with gestures, expressions and nodding – physical feedback.

Verbal feedback works well also. Here's how it's **not** done:

"I've had a bad day."

"You sound like you've had a bad day today."

"Uh, yes – I flunked a test."

"Oh my, you flunked a test!"

"Right. I guess I didn't study hard enough."

"You just didn't study hard enough – I hear you."

When you teach active listening (which you should), you will likely hear something like this when your students start practicing. The resulting laughter will make for a fun session, but you will want to be prepared to show how to do it properly, or they may never learn the skill. Active listening should sound more like this:

"I've had a bad day."

"I'm sorry – tell me about it."

"I flunked a test."

"Ouch! That must hurt. What subject?"

"Math, I guess I didn't study hard enough."

"That could do it."

With active listening, your responses should reflect that you actually heard the speaker, but without coming across like a parrot. Comments should not be critical, and you should avoid steering the conversation to yourself or to anything else – let the other person finish what they are saying.

Does this make sense?

When it's your turn to be the speaker, how can you tell that you are being understood? If the other person is doing active listening, you will know that they are understanding what you are saying, and you will be able to quickly spot when communication stops (because the feedback will suddenly stop making sense).

If the listener is not practicing active listening, it is up to you to somehow figure out if you were understood.

Try to avoid the traditional parental style: "Now repeat what I said."

I know the person may not have heard you, and you know they may not have heard you, but statements like that are condescending and express a huge lack of trust – thus they should be reserved for only the most serious occasions (where lack of understanding could jeopardize someone's safety).

Some better phrases are:

- "Am I making sense?"
- "Does this sound reasonable?"
- "Do you have any suggestions?"

While these phrases do not guarantee understanding, they do at least ensure that the person will at least briefly think about what you said – at least enough to try to respond. If all you get is a blank stare, you might want to start over. Or perhaps give up – let's face it, if a person really does not want to listen, there's not much point in talking in the first place.

Now that's a lesson worth teaching to your group.

30 - Ask permission to offer advice

Adults just love to offer advice. Teens often respond to this by not listening. Curiously enough, so do most adults.

The problem is that offering unsolicited advice is largely a waste of time for all concerned. So unless it has to do with the rules or a health and safety issue, try to avoid offering advice unless asked for it.

If you do have some advice that you just can't resist sharing, go up to the individual or group and say something like this:

"I have some advice that I think will help. Can I share it with you?"

If they say no, walk away. If you want, in parting say: "No problem, if you change your mind let me know". But trust me, most of the time they will want to hear the advice (if only because of the fear they may be missing something important). And in a remarkable feat of verbal ju-jitsu, by asking this question you have placed them in the position of asking for your advice. Which means they will actually listen and consider it!

Encourage your group leaders to use this technique, especially when offering advice to individuals. As leaders of the group, it is less applicable for them to do so when working with groups, because offering advice and direction is an expected part of their job. But as the adult advisor, you should use this technique both for groups and individuals.

31 - Explore options, but leave the decision with them

One of the greatest compliments I ever received came from a teen I had been working with for several years. He was almost puzzled when he explained that any time he came to me for an answer to a simple problem, he seemed to end up with a much more complex problem – and many more answers to choose from.

As a youth advisor, it's not your job to make things easy on the teens. On the contrary – since people learn from challenges, it is perfectly fine for you to challenge them. One of the best ways to do this is to help them see facets of problems and options that they may not have otherwise considered. Here's an example:

"We're going to play capture the flag. Do you think we should eat before or after?"

"Capture the flag sounds like fun.. What time will you be playing?"

"We were thinking of meeting at 11."

"Sounds good... lots of exercise. Is there a water fountain at the park?"

"I think so... I suppose we could get drinks ahead of time..."

"Maybe pick them up when you go to eat? Are there places nearby to eat?"

"There's a supermarket not far away. They have a deli."

"That could work. How much do sandwiches cost there?"

"Uh... I guess I can call and find out."

".. and let people know. Sounds good. What's the weather forecast like?"

"Uh... I can check. Hopefully good, but if it rains we could catch a movie."

"Or maybe rent a movie and go to a house if you didn't get a chance to tell people to bring money?"

"Yeah, maybe. Or maybe we can tell people to bring old clothes and just play in the mud."

"That could be fun. If you do that could you make sure to bring some plastic bags or something? I don't want a bunch of wet and dirty teens in my car after the event."

"Sure, no problem."

The conversation started with simple problem – should the group eat before or after the game. But before the conversation ended, the event planner had to consider a variety of issues, ranging from the fact that tired players would want a drink, to the logistics of the meal, to researching the weather and food costs, to making sure attendees brought enough money, to having a backup plan in case of rain. At no point in the conversation was the teen actually told to do anything – nor did the advisor make a single decision.

Well, actually the advisor made one decision – insisting on his own right to keep his car clean. But that's a personal decision on the part of the advisor, and not a decision for the group. As an advisor, you always have the right to control your own actions.

Notice how the advisor pointed out the option of going to a house to see a movie only to have it "rejected" by the teen in favor of playing in the rain. This is a good thing – it shows that the teen is making independent decisions. If the teen just accepts your advice blindly, that means you are making the decisions, and you have some work to do.

What do you do if you find teens just following whatever option you bring up? Simple: bring up multiple options and force them to choose between them (staying neutral as to which one might be your own preference). Once they get used to choosing among options you present, it is a fairly short step to coming up with their own options (see Chapter 40 on creativity).

32 - Be explicit

Teens are not mind readers.

Let's say you've asked some teens to do a job because you think they are particularly capable of handling it. You might think that asking them to do the job is enough to communicate your confidence in their ability. After all, you wouldn't ask if you thought they couldn't do it, right? Your confidence is implied.

But when working with teens, implications are not enough.

If you are confident in them, say so explicitly.

When coming back from the beach, you might expect them to wipe the sand off their feet before getting in your nice clean car. After all, that is common courtesy. But common courtesy is learned, and some teens have not learned it yet – or more likely, they are so focused on something else that they simply forget for a while. So be explicit as to your expectations.

If you want teens to know what you are thinking, how you are feeling, what you expect of them, or anything else, don't rely on them to figure it out based on subtle hints or just your actions. Be clear. Be explicit.

And once you've said what you want to say, stop saying it. Teens will interpret constant repetition as condescension or as an indication that you don't trust them (which it is).

33 - Explain every decision

Hopefully you are allowing the teens you are working with to make their own decisions. But there will be times when you have to make decisions – especially when it comes to health and safety issues, or issues relating to the rules or policies of your organization. At those times it is important that you don't just decide, but explain your decisions – especially if the answer is "no". For example:

You are chaperoning a group of teens who are eating at a restaurant. Two teens come up to you and the following conversation takes place:

"Can we go across to street to the ice cream shop?"

"No."

"Come on – don't you think we can cross the street safely?"

"No, I mean..."

"We're not going to get in trouble or get kidnapped. Why can't we go?"

"Because I say so"

Ouch.

When working with teens, the answers "because", "just because", "because I said so" and all similar variations are terrible answers when it comes to developing leadership skills. Why?

- They invoke your authority instead of allowing them to be the leaders.
- They teach the lesson that authority is sufficient for leading or making decisions.
- They do not help the teen understand anything about your thought process in making the decision, so they can't learn from it.

Here's one way the conversation could have gone:

"Can we go across to street to the ice cream shop?"

"Let me think for a moment... No, not this time."

"Come on – don't you think we can cross the street safely?"

"I'm sure you can cross the street safely. It's not that at all. It has to do entirely with my responsibility as an advisor."

"Huh? What do you mean?"

"You see, I'm the only chaperone here. So if you go to the ice cream shop and something happens, not only would it take me a while to get there, I'd have to leave the group here – which would be irresponsible of me. If we had a second chaperone, I could let you go and still be acting responsibly."

"Oh... Next time we'll see if we can get a parent to come along."

The difference in approach starts from the initial response. By pausing and thinking about what they said, you are demonstrating respect and setting an example for them as leaders to use when other teens come to them with issues.

Explaining your reasoning works on many levels:

- It serves as an excellent example they can use when facing similar situations in the future.

- It shows that you are not being arbitrary, but do actually consider requests carefully – a good way to earn respect.

- It demonstrates confidence in their ability to understand the issues involved.

- It frames the decision as a question of how you choose to do your job instead of on their actions or whether or not you trust them.

- It offers an alternative for the future – a way for them to get a "yes" answer next time.

But what if you don't have a good reason? What if you just do not want them to leave and you don't have a logical reason? That's OK. Here's an example:

I was traveling with a small group of teens and we were in a long security line at the airport without a great deal of time to spare. Two of them wanted to leave the line for just a few minutes to check out something in a shop. I had no logical reason not to let them go; but I was quite stressed over the time and just didn't want to deal with the extra stress of worrying about whether they might not get back by the time we moved up in the line. So my response was exactly that:

"No! Sorry people. I am really stressed about getting us through security and I just can't handle us being split up right now. Hopefully there will be shops and some time once we get through security."

There are two things to note about that response. First, it started with a very clear and absolute "No!" I really was stressed at the time and I assure you there was nothing iffy, weak or uncertain about that no. It was as firm and final as they come without actually yelling. And since I did not have any good reason, I explained my lack of reason. It's OK to be human, and it's ok on occasion to remind the teens that you are human. In fact, it's important that you do so, because if you can accept and acknowledge your own flaws it will give them permission and freedom to accept and acknowledge theirs.

34 - Don't yell

One of the most remarkable and perplexing parts of human communication is the way that volume works. When speaking, we tend to believe that increasing volume helps people to hear better. In fact, when traveling in foreign countries, many a tourist has instinctively acted as if speaking loudly and slowly enough will allow anyone to understand you, even if they do not understand a word of the language you are speaking.

In reality, the only time that volume helps with communication is when the listener has a legitimate hearing loss. For everyone else (teens in particular), increasing the volume seems to have the reverse effect on understanding. The louder you speak, the less they hear.

The solution is counter-intuitive, but very effective.

Speak softly.

If you speak more softly, people have to concentrate to hear you. If they are concentrating on hearing you, they may actually hear what you are saying.

One variation of this technique can work well when calling out names, perhaps to divide people into groups or check who is on a bus. Instead of shouting the names, say them quietly and quickly. People are sensitive to their names, so going through a list quietly and quickly twice can be more effective than doing so loudly and slowly.

Some people yell when they are angry. Some people get quieter. Guess which ones are more effective at getting their point across?

When teaching this technique to teens, the message and lesson changes a bit. When you yell at the teens, it comes across not as leadership, but as a parent yelling at a child. But when a teen leader yells at his or her peers, it obviously won't be perceived that way. It is important to be sensitive to the fact that individuals have different leadership styles – some teens do well by yelling, others can lead well without raising their voice. The two key lessons to teach them are these:

- Stress to them that there are many effective leadership styles, and they should choose one that suits them. You may find that one teen tries to use a technique that he or she has seen used effectively by someone else, and becomes very upset that it doesn't work well for them.

- Stress to the teens that even when they have developed a leadership style that works for them, it is important to learn how to use other techniques as well. For example: a quiet leader can have a large impact by occasionally yelling, just as a leader who yells a lot can be effective by sometimes becoming very quiet.

35 - Choose your battles

Have you ever played whack-a-mole at an amusement park midway? Each time you whack one of the moles, another one pops its head out.

Working with a group of teens is just like a whack-a-mole game. Just when you think that you've addressed all of the issues or problems, something new pops up to challenge you.[12]

There is one crucial difference between the amusement park game and a teen group: In whack-a-mole, all of the moles have the same value. But not every problem teens face is equally important.

You have a certain amount of time, resources and credibility available. If you take a whack at every problem that comes up, you will have a very hard time being effective. If you've made a huge fuss over a minor issue, the teens might be sick of hearing from you when something major comes along. You may find yourself spread too thin – unable to pay adequate attention to the issues at hand. You might even burn out.

So it is critically important to choose your battles carefully.

Here are some general guidelines you can use when deciding whether to get involved:

---

[12] And to make things even more fun: once you have a group functioning smoothly and all the teens trained and educated, they go off and graduate and you have to start all over again with beginners.

- Can the teens handle the problem on their own? Sometimes it means sitting back and waiting a bit to see if they recognize the problem and can act on it. They may take longer than you would, but that's often OK.
- Is the issue really important? Is it a safety issue? A group of teens may get loud and annoying, and may even be annoying people around them – but that doesn't mean you should step in. Set the threshold for action to limit your involvement as much as you can.

If you do get involved, use the least amount of intervention you can. If it is an emergency, obviously it may be necessary for you to speak up forcefully. But otherwise you will likely have the time to pull one or two of the teens aside, explain your concerns, and help them to become aware of and deal with the issue. In fact, it is by expecting and helping them to address problems that they learn the most.

And if, when you bring the problem to their attention, you find that they don't see it as a problem, think about it before you react. They may well be right.

Most adults tend to assume that they know better than teenagers on almost any issue. In truth, adults do tend to recognize problems, evaluate them, and respond to them better than teens – that's a result of experience. But if your purpose is to help teens develop those skills, you have to learn to step back as much as possible and allow them the opportunity to recognize, evaluate, and respond to issues on their own. It is possibly the hardest part of developing teen leaders.

Here's an example from some time back:

I was chaperoning an event with multiple youth group chapters – maybe 100 teens (including about 15 from our group, several of whom were new members). After ice skating, groups drove off to a nearby restaurant. There was a certain amount of chaos, and I found myself left behind in the parking lot with the new members who had been forgotten, and without enough spaces in my car to take the entire group. Some of them also needed to get home, and did not have time to eat out. I was actually quite angry with the teen leaders – who should have taken responsibility to make sure everyone in their group had rides and permission to stay out and eat (and they definitely should not have driven off without checking with me first). After ultimately making our way to the restaurant, I had to figure out how to respond.

This was an important issue, and there was some urgency in that some of the teens had to get home. But it was not an emergency. I sat in the car for a few minutes and forced myself to calm down. Then I went inside, found the chapter president and vice president and firmly asked them to join me outside.

I then described what happened, and pointed out the immediate issue that some of their members needed to get home. Though I spoke quietly and calmly, they knew I was upset not just because of my expression, but because I was explicit and told them how I felt.

My final comment to them was "That's the situation. You have a problem. Fix it."

I then turned around and returned to my car to cool off some more.

About 10 minutes later the entire group came out. They had decided that the way to solve the problem was for the entire group to head home – thus making sure that those who needed to get home did so on time. It wasn't the only possible solution – but it's the one they picked, and it was a good one.

Reading this story you might wonder how it was possible for the situation to come up in the first place. Why didn't I remind the leaders ahead of time to keep an eye on the new members, or check if someone needed to be home early? In fact, why weren't they trained properly as to the responsibilities of leadership – the need to take care of the entire group and not just themselves? And why didn't I notice when some of them drove off, even though the situation was chaotic?

Why? Because this happened many years ago when I was younger, less experienced, and had been with the group for only a few months. This kind of scenario is much less likely now – in part because of the lessons I learned that evening.

Guess what – you will make mistakes. You will pick the wrong battles. You will handle them poorly. But if you admit your mistakes and learn from them, you'll do better – and in doing so, will set an example for the teen leaders who need to learn these techniques as well.

36 - Mistakes and failure

You are not the only one who is going to make mistakes. As mentioned in Part I, giving teens the opportunity to make mistakes and learn from them in a safe and controlled environment is one of the reasons most youth organizations exist.

This means you'll find yourself dealing with the teens' mistakes in several different ways:

- Helping teens deal with their own mistakes.
- Dealing as an advisor with their mistakes.
- Helping teen leaders deal with the mistakes of other teens.

Let's look at these one at a time.

Helping teens deal with their own mistakes

When we make mistakes or fail at something, we feel lousy. That's human nature. Hopefully, after making a mistake, we take the time to remember all the things we did right. It's important, after a failure, to remember our successes. These strengthen us, restore our self-esteem, and give us the fortitude to face our mistakes, learn from them, and move on.

Of course, this sounds easier than it is. Even as adults it is not unusual for mistakes or failures to leave us feeling down, frustrated, disappointed and angry. For teens it is even more difficult, as they often do not have a strong history of success needed to counter the failure. Or put another way, they can be far harder on themselves than a situation actually merits.

That's where you come in. As an advisor, you can offer that sense of perspective and balance. You can point out where things went right. You can differentiate between failures of judgment and failures due to circumstances and bad luck.

Most of all, you can help the teen find ways to deal with the issue – whether it is by apologizing or making amends, or coming up with a plan to deal with the revised situation, or preparing and looking forward to a future attempt or project. Above all, you can help them learn from that mistake or failure, understand why it occurred, and give them the confidence that those mistakes won't be repeated.

There will also be times when, no matter how obvious it is to you and everyone else around you, the teen will refuse to acknowledge or accept that they made a mistake. In these cases you can try to raise their awareness and point it out to them, but there's a good chance it won't work. If so, you will most likely end up having to agree to disagree on the issue. You generally cannot help someone who does not want help, and you cannot help someone learn from a mistake that they do not recognize as one.

Dealing with their mistakes

There will be times when you will watch teens say or do things, and your reaction will be absolute astonishment that any human being can be so clueless. You will see failures in judgment so spectacular that you will wonder if their brain is functioning at all. And you will witness the kind of mistakes that are generally made by leading politicians caught in a truly great political scandal.

Most of the time you'll be able to deal with mistakes as described in the previous section, but sometimes the nature of the mistake will require you to take action – particularly if the mistake involved a violation of the organizations rules or policies, or if it endangered someone.

Consider this example:

One teen has been teasing and provoking another all evening. Suddenly, the second one loses his temper and throws the first one to the ground. They fight briefly until they are pulled apart by the other teens. How do you deal with this kind of situation – one that would almost certainly represent a rules violation in any youth group?

It's a tricky question. Fighting is not acceptable; so you can't just ignore it. Do you kick it up to your supervisor to deal with, knowing that one or both of the teens may face serious consequences or punishment? Do you apply some sort of punishment directly (if your organization permits it)? Do you talk to one of them, or both of them?

Let's start with a basic premise:

You should not feel that you have to deal with any issue that you are truly uncomfortable handling. In other words, if you aren't prepared to deal with a situation yourself, you should absolutely pass the buck up to your supervisor who is hopefully more experienced. This will be more common for newer or younger youth advisors, but even the most experienced of us will call in reinforcements when needed.

Here's how I handled that particular situation (note that by this time I was already a very experienced advisor):

- I started with an investigation. I spoke with the two teens and eyewitnesses to make sure I had a good understanding of what happened.
- I spoke with the first teen (the one who had provoked the other, but was hit first) and asked him to be patient while I addressed the issue, and that we would talk again soon.
- Over the next couple of days I spoke with the second teen, first to make it clear that no matter what the

provocation, a physical attack was unacceptable. This was important, because at first he felt his actions were justified. Ultimately, I had to make it clear to him that if he did not come to understand that it was a mistake, I would have to pass the incident up to the next level (which would involve parents and my supervisor).

- Once he understood the severity of the situation, we came up with a set of consequences. The first was that he had to apologize to the first teen. He also had to apologize to the entire group (remember, this had taken place in public). Finally, he had to plan an anger management program for the group.

- At the same time, I reframed the nature of these consequences. They were no longer "punishment". Instead, they became ways to improve the group – to teach others valuable skills. In addition, they put him in a visible leadership position. In other words, the "consequences" were designed in every way to build him up, to restore and increase his stature with the group, and to help him learn new skills by requiring him to teach those skills to others. Instead of being an adversary, I was now his teacher and ally – helping him to recover from a serious mistake.

- Next, I arranged a lunch with him, the first teen and myself during which he apologized and they had a chance to discuss the situation. At that time we also discussed the provocation issue, and the first teen came to realize that what he considered harmless ribbing was being taken far more seriously than he knew.

Did it work? I don't recall if the two ever became particularly good friends, but they got along. The second teen never got into another fight. In fact, he was later elected chapter president.

When the teens make a mistake or experience a failure, always ask yourself how you can help them to learn from the situation. Try to find a way to make it clear to them that you are on their side – because that's where you're supposed to be.

Helping teens deal with other people's mistakes or failures

As you've just read, facing mistakes and learning from them is the best way to deal with most mistakes and failures – and this is a lesson you can teach teen leaders both explicitly and through example.

There are some issues that tend to come up very frequently when teens try to deal with the mistakes of other teens and adults.

First, there is a tendency to expect perfection – particularly from people in authority. If a parent, advisor, or other teen leader makes a mistake, they sometimes react very strongly with anger, disappointment or disillusionment. They may see a simple human mistake as hypocrisy or corruption.[13] It is important for you to remind them that nobody is perfect, and particularly important to remind them that you aren't perfect.

Second, there is a tendency to attribute to malice what is usually nothing more than miscommunication or lack of

---

[13] This is not, I regret to say, unique to teenagers. It is a state of affairs that has become endemic in our society. For evidence of this, just watch how the media portrays any government official, elected or not, should anything go wrong (regardless of whether they had any control over the matter, or ability to influence the outcome).

consideration. A good technique here is to brainstorm possible reasons for the other person's actions. Could they have been feeling sick or tired? Could they have been so focused on other issues that they simply did not consider some factor?

Helping teens to see each other as people rather than as roles (and helping them to see you as a person rather than as a title) will go a long way to helping the group become one where individual differences are well tolerated.

37 - Get help

Teens generally hate asking for help. Yet asking for help is a fundamental part of leadership. Only a boss can dictate to other people. A leader has to inspire – to call others to join them – to ask for help.

There are two ways to teach this skill. First, set the example. Don't be afraid to ask for help yourself. In fact, don't be afraid to ask the teens for help – they will take it as a compliment.

Second, find opportunities to explain why asking for help is characteristic of good leaders. Here are some points you can make:

- It is far better to ask for help than to fail. You don't lose credit for a success just because you had help along the way.
- Asking for help gains you allies (and helps build friendships). When you ask someone for help, you are expressing trust and confidence in them.
- Asking for help improves the group. The people who help you will also gain new experience and become stronger leaders.

If you find individuals very resistant to the idea of asking for help, try positioning it as "teamwork" instead. It is not quite the same thing, but is close enough to move things in the right direction if you find yourself with a group of stubborn individualists.

Beyond asking for help is the issue of delegation. Teen leaders (like many adults) often have a tendency to try to do everything themselves, figuring (often correctly) that the only way to be sure something is done properly is to do it themselves. Yet delegation is one of the most powerful techniques a leader has available, as it potentially allows a leader to accomplish far more than is possible by one person acting alone. Delegation offers the opportunity to manage projects and people, and to develop skills that MBA students spend thousands of dollars to learn in school. It also offers the opportunity to learn how to deal with people who fail to complete tasks delegated to them (which, in a group of teens will happen fairly often). In fact, there are so many lessons to be learned through the process of delegation that you may find it one of the major issues you deal with.

38 - Group problem solving

Many youth groups include some form of self-government. This aspect of leadership has not been emphasized in this book partly because you can take it for granted, but more importantly, because leadership is not inherent in an office. Electing someone to an office does not make them a leader – it just gives them the opportunity to develop and exercise leadership skills. By the same token, an individual with strong leadership skills can have a huge impact on a group without being elected to any office.[14]

One task that leaders, in particular elected leaders, are likely to face is that of solving a problem or making a decision as a group. Some groups have informal decision making processes; others adopt various forms of parliamentary procedure. Regardless of the particular format, group problem solving should always incorporate the following steps:

1. **Define the problem.** This is not just a matter of stating the problem – it also involves seeking agreement from the group that the problem actually exists. You can't get people to join in solving a problem that they do not believe exists in the first place.

2. **Brainstorming solutions**. In a brainstorming session, one or two people write down ideas that are contributed by everyone in the group. The rules of brainstorming are that any idea is welcome and no

---

[14] This is, by the way, an important philosophy to share with the group – particularly for encouraging teens who don't hold an office, or have just lost an election, to remain involved and continue to take initiative with the group. It's also an important message for teen leaders to hear to encourage them to keep non-elected individuals engaged.

commentary, evaluation or criticism of ideas is allowed. The purpose of a brainstorming session is to allow a free flow of creative ideas without fear that your ideas will be dismissed.

3. **Discussion**. During this phase the group discusses the pros and cons of various solutions and chooses a solution to adopt.

4. **Determine Success Criteria.** The group should also establish a way to judge whether a solution succeeded and a time to meet again to evaluate the results of the solution. This step is important, but is often neglected.

5. **Evaluation.** At the time specified in step 4, the group should evaluate the effectiveness of the solution. If the solution was unsatisfactory, return to step 2 or 3 and try another approach.

If your group uses parliamentary procedure, you may need to emphasize problem definition and brainstorming. Parliamentary procedure only deals with step 3 – and there is a tendency of groups that use it to go directly to proposing and discussing solutions without truly considering the nature of the problem they want to solve.

39 - Principles of leadership

Before you can teach leadership to teens, it is important that you yourself understand leadership: what it is, how and why certain techniques work, and above all – the difference between good leadership and bad leadership (as compared to effective and ineffective leadership). This chapter discusses the principles of leadership and a variety of leadership techniques. The material in this chapter can also be used to teach leadership techniques to the teens you work with.

Good vs. effective leadership

People often confuse good leadership with effective leadership – but it is an important distinction.

An effective leader is one who is able to make things happen – to drive change in an organization. When an effective leader makes a decision, the group follows. They follow even if they are being led off a cliff.

This brings us to the difference between good and bad leadership. A good leader acts to the benefit of the community – placing the needs of others equal or above their own. A poor leader acts in their own self-interest. There are other aspects of good and bad leadership, but this is the heart of it.

Here is an example I use when I talk about good leadership:

Many youth groups have regional or even national conventions. The chapters in our area were boarding a bus to go to one of these conventions. Unfortunately, due to "problems" with both the bus company and our region's management, the bus was a few seats short – so we needed to have a parent quickly drive a few teens to another bus that had a stop about a half hour away. One of the teens we were going to send to the other bus was a newer member of our group who had made a mistake in his registration and thus had not been assigned a seat on our bus.

As we were about to send him off, the president of our chapter came to me and asked permission to go in his stead, saying that it was more important that the younger member ride the bus to his first convention.

Just think about it. He was willing to give up the bus ride with his own chapter in order to allow a new member that opportunity. Why was this a demonstration of excellent leadership? He saw a problem. He came up with a solution. He placed the needs of the community ahead of his own. It's no wonder he was elected president of the chapter.

Leadership is a skill set

Some teens are "natural leaders". But what does that really mean?

We often use the term natural leader to describe someone who is charismatic – who others admire and follow. Just because someone is charismatic does not mean that actually know what it takes to be a strong leader or that they have real leadership skills. It just means that some leadership skills come naturally to them.

Leadership skills – that's the key phrase. Exercising leadership requires a set of skills that anyone can learn. This entire part of the book is full of leadership skills that teens can learn. And in learning them, even teens that are not particularly charismatic can turn into very strong leaders. In time, a day comes when they wake up to discover (to their absolute astonishment) that they have become charismatic and popular without even realizing it. I've seen it happen often.

Leadership is a choice

I mentioned in Chapter 38 that leadership is not inherent in an office. Winning an election or being appointed to an office does not make someone a leader. Leadership is a choice you make. It is a choice anyone can make.

Part of your job as an advisor is to encourage this choice and to make sure that the group does not dismiss members who want to get involved just because they do not have a title.

In the youth group I work with, it is very clear that there are two leadership tracks. There are those who run for office and take on the responsibilities of running the chapter. And there are those who are more project oriented – who prefer to plan events or activities rather than hold an office. This "project" track offers extraordinary leadership opportunities as well. Our first cross-country trip (to Washington D.C.) was planned by a couple of 8th graders who had just joined the chapter and had not yet even had a chance to run for a chapter office.

Role Modeling

People often think leadership is giving speeches or arguing points. Teens are especially likely to think this way, as those are the specific actions that are typically pointed out when they are told that someone is a leader. However, the single most effective leadership technique is actually in setting a good example. Being a good role model is by far the most important leadership technique to teach and to learn.

How do you teach this concept?

First and foremost, by being a good role model yourself. In all of your interactions with the teens (or even with adults when the teens are watching), you should act as you would hope they would act. Make no mistake – they will be watching you closely. They will hear every word you say (and will quote back to you statements later that you won't even remember making).

Even as you teach youth leadership, and encourage the teens to take on leadership roles – even if you reach the point of nirvana where the teens are completely in charge and responsible for their group and you have no leadership role beyond being a chaperone – even then, it is essential that you model good leadership.

Then, when you talk about the importance of being a role model, you can (and should) credibly point to your own actions.

Leaders can't control people

Teens often believe that leaders have the ability to control people. After all, what is the purpose of leadership if not to somehow have control?

But this is fundamentally wrong. You cannot control other people – especially in a youth group where participation is largely voluntary. You can only influence people through your own actions.

When teen leaders get frustrated because they are unable to get people to agree with them, or follow their lead, they naturally tend to blame others. And in fact, they may be right – the other members may be completely to blame. But it does not matter – the only tools a leader has to change the situation is their willingness and ability to modify their own behavior.

So if one approach does not work, a leader has to try other approaches (even if the rest of the members are being totally unfair or unreasonable).

This concept also applies when advising teens on how to deal with parents who they see as unreasonable. Explain to them that it doesn't matter if their parents are wrong or right – the only way they can influence their parents is through their own choices and actions. If whining and complaining does not work, they need to try something else.

Other leadership techniques

Every leader has a "bag of tricks" – leadership skills and techniques that can be used for various purposes. Here's a shopping list of techniques you can teach that are effective and easy to use and understand. They are also techniques that you can and should use yourself.

Getting people quiet

It can be hard to get a group of teens quiet. Most teen leaders trying to get people quiet will start by yelling for quiet. While this will work occasionally for smaller groups, yelling (making more noise) is not the most effective way to get a group quiet.

The best way to get a group quiet is to recruit a few of the other teens ahead of time and ask them to, when prompted, keep themselves quiet and, without speaking, keep those next to them quiet. Then the leader can stand in front of the group, signal (quietly) for people to pay attention, and rely on the teen leaders spread out through the group to quietly spread the word and get those near them to pay attention. This approach can work even for large groups. If you prepare your assistants properly and they spread themselves out, this technique cannot fail.

Don't take credit, give credit

It is common for teens who are working to become leaders to try to take credit for their work. This is understandable. Who doesn't want to be acknowledged for their efforts? But it turns out that giving credit and acknowledging the effort of others is a much stronger leadership technique. There are two reasons for this:

- Everyone wants to have their work acknowledged, so when you acknowledge someone they will think highly of you – making them more likely to listen to you and follow you in the future.
- Who gives someone the "right" to acknowledge someone? Usually it is the person in charge – the leader – who gives credit. So, if you stand up and acknowledge someone, that must mean you have the authority to do so. Right? In other words, you position yourself as a leader by giving credit to others.

The same applies to compliments in general. In what is a kind of interpersonal head fake, the more you give credit and acknowledge others, the stronger you appear as a leader.

Admit your mistakes

Sometimes leaders get the idea that they cannot show any weakness, and must be perfect, in order to be effective. These teens get into trouble when things go wrong. They may try denial, deception, avoidance and various other approaches to maintain the illusion that they did nothing wrong. Of course, everyone sees through this and it ultimately harms their reputation as a leader.

It is far better to stand up and admit mistakes, apologize and resolve to do better. Teens understand mistakes (often better than adults). Because admitting a mistake is so hard, those who do it are seen as courageous; and the admission can serve to increase their stature as leaders.

Of course, if someone is making many mistakes, constantly admitting them does not negate the fact that the mistakes were made in the first place – but that is a different kind of problem.

Look for the good

People find what they look for. If you look for problems, you will see them everywhere. If you look for the worst in people, you will find everyone lacking.

However, if you look for the good, you will find that as well. There are few people for whom you cannot find and acknowledge something positive.

A good leader does not ignore the bad things and the problems. But a good leader does seek out the good in the group and in individuals. A good leader looks for successes as well as problems, and points those successes out so that everyone can see them.

Ask questions

Some teens (and many adults) follow the credo that it is better to remain silent and be a fool than to ask a question and let everyone know that you are a fool.

That is a foolish credo indeed.

Asking questions is the mark of a good leader. For one thing, if you ask questions you might end up actually knowing something. In addition, when you ask someone a question you are giving them a compliment – engaging them in the topic at hand. In other words – acting like a leader.

One of the best ways to teach this skill is through example. Be sure to ask the teens questions, especially before offering advice. And make sure some of those questions are "stupid" questions. When the teens laugh, smile confidently and explain to them that there is no such thing as a stupid question.

Part III - Programs and Activities

Every youth organization holds activities of various kinds. From the perspective of developing youth leadership, these programs and activities are all important. It is in the planning and execution of these activities that teens have the greatest opportunity to learn and practice leadership skills.

This means, of course, that part of your job will consist of teaching the teens how to plan and execute programs.

Even a typical youth activity, like going bowling or to the movies, can offer leadership opportunities. Teens can be involved in researching the activity, budgeting for it, creating the schedule, arranging transportation, promoting attendance and ultimately leading it (directing others, making announcements, and so forth). Did I say involved? In fact, it is possible for the teens to plan and execute the entire event with no adult involvement whatsoever. With the group I work with (which has highly skilled leaders), my involvement typically consists of one phone call or email in which they brief me as to what is going on, I ask one or two questions, and that's it until I (or designated staff) show up at the event.[15] In fact, the only times I have to pay more than cursory attention to event planning are higher risk activities, or complex programs like a trip or weekend retreat.

The reason I emphasize this is that adults have a tendency to underestimate what teens are actually capable of when given the chance. I still have that tendency, even though time

---

[15] If the event is as simple as going to a movie, it most likely would be planned by a 13 or 14 year old under the supervision of one of the older leaders.

and again I see teens accomplish tasks that many adults could not handle. I recall the time when one of our high school juniors came up to me and declared that he was going to plan a group trip to Japan. I was able to keep a straight face and say suitably encouraging things, though I had some serious doubts (as you could imagine). But over the next few months he did a great deal of research, recruited additional staff, and found parents who traveled frequently who could donate some frequent flyer miles help cover the transportation costs. Six months later I was on a plane with two other staff and 11 teenagers, heading off to an amazing week in Tokyo. Yes, I did double check the arrangements, and did some additional research behind the scenes to make sure I understood the plans and contingencies. I also provided guidance in terms of material that needed to be prepared – like parent packets, and emergency contact phone trees. But all of the real work and planning was handled by the teen. And he did all of the work on the trip itself: checking us into the hotels, instructing us on which rail passes to buy, waking us up in the morning, and navigating us through the complex Tokyo subway system.

So when a teen tells you that they can do something, give them the benefit of the doubt – you never know what could happen.

40 - Creativity

Every event or program starts with an idea.

When you or a group leader challenges someone to come up with an idea for an activity or program, I guarantee that sooner or later (probably sooner) you will hear: "I'm not creative" or "I don't have any good ideas".

I hate it when I hear those phrases from anyone – especially teens. To see creativity beaten out of them so young is tragic.

The good news is that, believe it or not, you can teach creativity. Yes, anyone can be creative – even you.

Here's the secret:

Creativity is not a personal characteristic – it is a skill. And it is a skill that you can learn.

You see, people who think they aren't creative believe that creative people have good ideas. This is absolutely not true. Creative people don't have good ideas. They just have lots and lots of ideas, most of which are pretty stupid.

A non-creative person, when looking for an idea, searches, thinks, and tries to come up with a good idea – and any glimmer of an idea that does not immediately look great is quickly killed. Their mind has a well honed filter – a screen that shreds all but the most amazing ideas. This screen is so powerful that almost no ideas are able to get through. It's no surprise these people remain silent and think they don't have any good ideas – any ideas, even those that might grow into good ideas, get killed long before they can be spoken.

A creative person lacks this filter. Their mind seethes with the most stupid and bizarre ideas that you can imagine. Many are politically incorrect. Some would shock you if you knew about them. When a creative person needs an idea, they allow all of these crazy ideas to flow past them, searching for those that have the potential to grow into something useful. They aren't as afraid of saying something stupid – because they know that stupid ideas can often inspire great ideas.

Or put another way: a creative person does not come up with good ideas; they come up with a lot of ideas and pick out the best of them.

If you're teaching creativity, after you've explained this concept, hold a brainstorming session in which you challenge the group to come up with the worst possible ideas for an event.

Then, choose some of the worst of them, and challenge them to come up with ways to turn them into good events.

I remember one time that we did this someone came up with the idea of spending the night in a graveyard digging up dead bodies. Once we all stopped laughing and thought more about it, the idea evolved into a Halloween event in which we re-created the funeral practices of different cultures. It was a great idea that never would have come to light if not for a demented zombie lover who had the courage to speak up.

Here's another useful technique: Don't stop with the first great idea. In other words – once the teens have come up with a good idea, encourage them to set it aside for a moment, and then see if they can come up with a second good idea. Then they can choose which one they like best.

41 - Types of programs

Programs and activities are a huge topic – one deserving of an entire book. In this section, I will cover some of the basics – the kinds of things I would teach the teens in a basic programming workshop.

While there are a huge number of possible programs and activities available to a group of teens, they all tend to fall into certain program types, each of which has its own characteristics, advantages and disadvantages.

Discussion programs

Small group discussions are best, though short discussions can work with a large group if you have one or two strong leaders. Small group discussions work best when people are sitting in circles, large groups (over 25 or so) usually require that everyone face the leaders.

Advantages:

- Discussions work with almost any subject. They are especially good for "mixer" type games.

Disadvantages:

- Tend to be overused.
- Often too "school" like. The only program type worse than discussions are lectures (which should be used rarely if ever).

Comments:

Timing is very important. Be sure to allow enough time for each person in the group to contribute (with small groups), and be ready to extend the time if things are going well. Also, be ready to move on if things start to drag.

In discussions where one person is acting as moderator, it is important that they not dominate the discussion, but allow others to speak with as much fairness as possible.

One hour for a discussion is probably the maximum at high school age. Half an hour is better.

Tricks:

- Having a co-leader for a discussion (or planting an assistant in the group) can help, especially if things are starting out slowly.

- When leading a program where a larger group is divided into smaller discussion groups, try to have one assistant in each group who is prepared to help facilitate the discussion, and who you can ask how things are going so that you can judge timing.
- Give the groups a 1-3 minute warning so that they have time to wrap things up.
- Leaders and small group leaders should prepare a list of discussion points or questions ahead of time. When using small discussion groups, provide your small group leaders or assistants a written list of discussion points or instructions.

Simulation programs

In this type of program, you simulate a historical or fictional event. Simulations usually involve doing some research and always involve a degree of role-playing. Classic examples include: Mock Congress, Prison Break / Underground Railroad, Future society.

Advantages:

- A successful simulation can be one of the most effective, fun, and otherwise great programs you can do. Perhaps more than any other type of program, it can make a "meaningful" or educational program fun. A properly planned simulation will rarely fail.

Disadvantages:

- Simulations are probably the most complex and difficult programs to pull off. They take the most preparation. They generally take a large staff. It is a good choice for team programming, or for one group to prepare for other groups.

Comments:

Preparation is everything. All of the people working on the program need to understand exactly what they need to do and when to do it. More than any other program, plans for a simulation should be written up in detail (with a complete description and schedule for the event).

Simulations need to be carefully designed for the age group. Simulations for older participants should be correspondingly more sophisticated.

Simulations tend to be long (especially the complex ones). Figure one to two hours for a simple one. Allow several hours or even a full day for a major simulation. They can be great on weekend retreats.

Tricks:

- The best way to make a simulation succeed is to have the people leading the program really get into it. A high energy level among those leading the program will encourage the participants to get involved as well.
- On a weekend retreat, you can incorporate one or more meals into the simulation.
- Be sure to review the simulation program carefully. Make sure activities are appropriate. For example: in an underground railroad simulation, you would likely allow for the possibility of escaping slaves to be caught, but you wouldn't want to simulate them being whipped. You might also want to discuss ahead of time what kind of language would be acceptable during the program – you probably would not want the simulation to include realistic language from the time (which is extremely racist by today's standards).
- Because they simulate reality, simulations can be more intense than other programs and can result in strong reactions on the part of participants. Encourage the program leaders to watch for participants who are uncomfortable or having trouble, and to keep you aware of any situations that develop.
- A simulation program should always have a debriefing session afterwards to discuss the program and make sure participants understood the point of the simulation.

Role-plays

These take many forms: from simple drama games to reenactments of historical events, to portrayals of various scenarios.

Advantages:

- Relatively easy to put together.
- Fun to do.
- Excellent for "soft" subjects such as values, ethics, dealing with feelings, personal experiences, and so forth.

Disadvantages:

- Tend to be light on content (A high informational content role-play effectively becomes a simulation).
- Works best in a "safe" (non-threatening) environment.

Comments:

A brief follow-up discussion is usually necessary to make the point of the program clear to all participants.

Tricks:

- Role-plays work best when the leaders are comfortable "acting out" - or acting a bit crazy. A demonstration by the leaders can help loosen participants up.

Round robin

In a round robin, a large group is divided into smaller groups. The small groups visit various "stations" where a part of the program takes place. After a short period of time, the groups rotate to the next station.

Round Robins combine very nicely with other program types - thus each station can have a discussion, role-play, speaker, or other activity.

Advantages:

- Perfect for dealing with various aspects of the same subject. Example: A round robin on village life might include a station on marriage, religion, business, and politics.
- Round robins tend to be resilient programs. The program can be very successful even if a couple of the stations are not outstanding.
- The combination of short programs tends to keep people's attention - even if their attention span is limited.

Disadvantages:

- Requires one or more leaders at each stations, plus people to keep time and keep the groups moving.
- Slightly harder to plan since it involves planning multiple small programs instead of one larger one.

Comments:

- A round robin is only as good as the various stations. The person planning the program needs to work closely with the station leaders and make certain that each station is prepared.

- Timing is crucial. Each station must be designed to take about the same amount of time.
- A total program length of one to two hours is typical.

Tricks:

- Be sure to schedule "movement" time between stations.
- Having a person whose job is to go from station to station telling groups to move on to the next station will help make things run smoothly. This person should also know where all the stations are.
- Let the station leaders get set up while dividing the large group into smaller groups.
- Each group should have a leader, or at least one person who knows where all the stations are.
- You can also rotate the station leaders and keep the groups stationary in cases where stations do not require advance setup.

Speakers

Outside speakers offer a great way to expose teens to information and perspective that they would not normally experience. Look beyond the obvious (famous people, athletes, celebrities) – some of your teens parents or neighbors may have interesting stories to share[16].

Advantages:

- Relatively easy to set up (though more complex for paid speakers or entertainers).
- Can be extremely successful and interesting if the speaker is good.

Disadvantages:

- This type of program is only as good as the speaker. If the speaker is bad, it can be a disaster.

Tricks:

- Talk to the speaker before the program. Make sure you both understand what the program is going to be about.
- Be sure the speaker knows how much time is available.
- Call beforehand to remind the speaker about the event, and to confirm that he or she will actually show up!

---

[16] One of the best speakers our group ever had was a parent who had served in the military in a special-forces branch.

Value auctions and related programs

This describes a very broad range of programs that encourage individuals or groups to form an idea or come to a decision. Examples include:

- Classic "values" auction in which values or principles are auctioned off as a means of allowing participants to decide which ones are most important to them.
- Spectrum activities in which individuals or groups place themselves physically between two extremes of opinion or value.
- Selection activities in which individuals or groups choose ideas or values, or set priorities.

These can be combined in many ways. Start by having individuals perform an activity then have them combine into groups based on their choices. Or start in small groups and have them work together in the activity. Or have individuals in a group adopt and defend different positions. Or have each group assigned an opinion or position. And so on...

Advantages:

- Adaptable to almost any subject.
- By combining other techniques (role-plays, cheers, presentations, and so forth) it is easy to develop a fun program.
- Lots of flexibility in terms of the amount of content to be included. It is possible, for example, to provide individuals or groups with resource material to use during the program.

Disadvantages:

- Requires a fair amount of preparation and organization.
- Works best with multiple leaders - perhaps even one for each group.

Tricks:

- Have a couple of teens or staff as floaters to help explain the program to those individuals or groups who find themselves confused or cannot follow instructions.
- Do not rely only on verbal instructions. Create handouts containing key information or instructions for the activity.
- Consider having a "no preference" or opt-out option. This is especially important when using this type of program with sensitive or personal issues, as you don't want individuals to be placed in a high-pressure or embarrassing situation.

Games

Games can take many forms, from group games to board games. Games can be combined with other program types such as role-plays or simulations. Games can have groups competing or individual participation. Don't neglect the possibility of adapting television game shows!

Games also serve well as mixers – programs that help members of a group to get acquainted or to know each other better. Many "improv" activities can be adapted as games.

Advantages:

- Adaptable to almost any subject.
- It is relatively easy to develop a fun program.
- Lots of flexibility in terms of the amount of content to be included.
- Excellent for mixers (especially the high-energy games).

Disadvantages:

- May require a fair amount of preparation and organization.

Tricks:

- If you are the game's MC (Master of Ceremonies), be sure you have an assistant available to help with various tasks such as keeping score and getting supplies.
- You can often help a game succeed by pre-selecting and preparing team leaders.

Mock events

These are a form of simulation. Mock trials and Model United Nations are classic examples of this type of event.

Advantages:

- Adaptable to many subjects.
- Lots of flexibility in terms of the amount of content to be included.

Disadvantages:

- May require a fair amount of preparation and organization.

Comments:

Mock trials can be played seriously (for serious issues), or can be given a fun and entertaining slant (with melodramatics, crazy judges, costumes and so on) for less serious issues.

Tricks:

- As program leader, you may wish to choose very strong people for key roles in the event. Example: In a trial, choose two strong participants to serve as attorneys.

Mini-courses

In this type of event, a large group is divided into smaller groups that address different subjects of interest. Each course can make use of many of the other program types and techniques. Mini-courses are similar to round-robins, except that each person only takes one or two of the courses, instead of spending a short amount of time at each station.

Advantages:

- Adaptable to many subjects.
- Lots of flexibility in terms of the amount of content to be included.
- Allows people to be involved in subjects that interest them.

Disadvantages:

- Requires at least one person for each course.

Tricks:

- Sign-up sheets that allow people to specify first and second choices have the advantage of allowing the organizers to divide people up more or less evenly among the courses offered.

Films

This includes watching films at a house, or going out to a theatre.

Advantages:

- Can be extremely effective.
- Quite popular as programs go.

Disadvantages:

- A largely passive activity with little social interaction.

Comments:

- Be sure to allow enough time for the film and (optionally) some discussion time.
- Best when people are at a low or moderate energy level (tired after an athletic event, late night or evening).

Tricks:

- If watching at a house, check the equipment beforehand.
- Consider organization and community standards when deciding how to respond if the teens want to show an 'R' Rated film.

Hikes, sports and other outdoor activities

In addition to traditional outdoor activities, you can creatively combine outdoor activities with other types of programs. For example: one successful event we had was a "back to grade school" day that included some crafts, naptime, milk and cookies, and traditional grade school games like dodge ball, jump-rope, hopscotch and four square.

Advantages:

- Can be a lot of fun.
- Quite popular.

Disadvantages:

- Rarely offers much in the way of content, though content can be added effectively by applying a bit of creativity.

Comments:

Logistics is important. Make sure you have any necessary supplies. Be sure people know what the event is so that they can dress appropriately and bring appropriate equipment (e.g. – shoes, water bottles for hike, safety equipment, etc.) Know where the nearest water and restrooms will be.

Arts and crafts

Be sure to think beyond traditional crafts using pens, paper, paint, paper and glue. Teens can undertake more ambitious projects such as building model rockets or wood and metal work. Seek out volunteer opportunities: paint a house, build a carnival booth and game, or build a house.[17]

Advantages:

- Can be a lot of fun.
- Can be tied in with content very effectively.

Disadvantages:

- Requires advanced preparation.

Comments:

Logistics is important. Make sure you have any necessary supplies.

Tricks:

- Sometimes guys have a hard time accepting that it's OK to do arts and crafts. And sometimes guys think they aren't creative so won't even try. You can overcome this by recruiting group leaders to participate enthusiastically and set an example.

---

[17] Teens 16 and over can work on a Habitat for Humanity construction site in most localities.

Trips and campouts

I have been on more trips and campouts as a youth group advisor than I can count. They have ranged from beach overnight campouts, to three or four day road trips staying in hotels or tents, to large trips across the country or abroad. There is no better way for a group to bond, and no better opportunity for members to form lasting friendships.

Advantages:

- Can be a lot of fun.
- Provides numerous opportunities for teens to gain leadership and planning skills.

Disadvantages:

- Relatively expensive.
- Relatively complex.
- Requires close monitoring by staff.

Comments:

Logistics is everything. As staff, you will need to verify transportation, lodging, adequate staffing, and compliance with your organization's policies and procedures. Plan on having more staff on a trip than you would have at a local activity.

Tricks:

- Bring an air mattress on campouts. I know it seems trivial. I could write a book on planning group trips and campouts at this point (and perhaps someday I will), but for now, of all the tips and tricks I've learned relating to this topic, none beats having an air mattress on an overnight or campout.

42 - Planning and logistics

Planning is necessary for all but the most trivial event. A plan helps you to prepare and run the event. But it is almost unheard of for an event or program to follow a plan exactly – so you have to be prepared for the unexpected.

Logistics is the military term for making sure that soldiers have what they need to fight: weapons, armor, food and drink. Good logistics can't win a war, but bad logistics can lose one.

The same applies to events and programs. Having the timing right, everyone prepared, and supplies on hand, will not guarantee that a program will succeed. But poor logistics – missing supplies, unprepared leaders, and poor scheduling – can ruin even the best designed program.

Here are a selection of guides and worksheets that you can use to help teens learn to plan programs:

Planning guide

Here is a rough sequence that goes into the planning of any event or activity (modify as necessary to fit your organization):

- **Get an idea for the event**: What? You don't have a good idea? No problem. Steal one. Borrow one. Ask other teens, parents, or your advisors. Brainstorm possibilities. Get creative.
- **Set vision and goals**: Try to build your idea into a rough outline for an event. What are your goals? What kinds of things would you like to see happen?
- **Run it by key people**: Once you have an idea, run it by your group leaders and advisors and see what they

think. Don't let them discourage you - but do listen for possible problems that they may see that you have missed. Run it by other teens as well, to get a feel for the interest level. (Note: some events will have immediate widespread support, but many excellent events will have strong support from only a few teens. Don't just go by the number of people who like the idea. However, if you get little or no support from anyone, the problem may be serious - discuss the situation further before proceeding.)

- **Revised planning**: Set a Date. Find a place. Revise your plans and maybe add some detail. How long will you need to prepare? Is it better for a Saturday or Sunday? Daytime or evening?

- **Detailed planning 1:** Come up with a tentative schedule and preliminary logistics. Decide what support you will need and who you might want to ask for help.

- **Marketing 1**: Start building group support and enthusiasm. Put out applications if necessary.

- **Detailed planning 2**: Sweat the details. Make lists of things to do and bring. Finalize the schedule of the event. Work out a planning schedule so that you can have everything done before the event. Make sure you have staff or chaperones.

- **Contingency planning**: Ask "what if" questions. What if it rains? What if a key person cancels? What if someone gets lost? Prepare backup plans for possibilities that seem likely or have serious consequences.

- **Marketing 2:** Put the word out on calls, emails, social networks or whatever other means you use to encourage people to attend. Don't forget the power of personal invitations.

- **Get the OK for the event**: Follow the procedure for your organization to finalize and approve the event.
- **The day before**: Check your lists to make sure you have everything you need. Lay it out in a place where you won't forget it. Call anyone helping out to make sure they are prepared. If they are supposed to bring things, make sure they have them ready. Call anyone else who you particularly want to encourage to attend.

Logistics worksheet

Time: When is the event?

- Do you have enough time for the things you wish to accomplish?
- Would the event work better during the day or at night?
- Did you allow time for transportation and people movement?
- For outdoor events, do you have a backup in case of poor weather?

Place:

- Do you have room for everyone?
- If splitting into groups, where will you put the different groups?
- When is the place available?
- Have you left time for cleanup (if necessary)?
- Are there any steps you should take ahead of time to prepare the place, or prepare people before using the place?

- If it is an overnight, do you have lodging?

Transportation:
- Do you have sufficient drivers?
- Have you allowed for transportation time?
- If the event involves a lot of travel, did you include funding to pay for gas?

Supplies:
- Do you have every possible supply that you think you will need?
- Did you make a list of supplies so that you won't forget any?

Staffing:
- Do you have the necessary number of staff or chaperones for the event?

Budget:
- Figure out your fixed costs and variable costs (see budgeting worksheet).
- How many people do you need to break even?
- When and how are you going to collect the money?

Bureaucracy:
- Are there any applications that need to be filled out or permits that need to be obtained?
- Do participants need to bring any documents such as student IDs or passports?
- Are there any required parental consent forms, liability waivers or medical releases?

Budgeting guide

You don't have to be a mathematician to budget chapter events (though some basic algebra doesn't hurt).

Price per person

This is the easiest kind of budgeting – where the cost of the event depends exactly on the number of people. An example of this would be a movie or miniature golf event, or eating out, where each person can pay their own way.

Price per group

Group costs are much harder to deal with. Let's say you have rented an entire ice-rink for a one-hour game of Broomball[18] for, say $200. How much do you tell each person to bring? If you budget for 20 people, it's $10 each. As long as 20 or more show up, you're fine (you can return the extra cash or maybe use it towards pizza after the event). But what happens if a bunch of people don't show up? It's not an easy problem, but here are some hints that will help:

- Budget for the worst-case turnout – not what you actually expect.
- Consider sign-ups with advance payment, only refundable if someone takes the place of a cancellation.
- Remember to ask for group discounts and non-profit discounts (if applicable) ahead of time.

Pizza

Sometimes your budgeting involves both pricing per person and per group. Examples of this are hotel rooms and pizza. Both hotel rooms and pizzas can support a certain

---

[18] Think ice hockey with rubber balls instead of pucks, brooms instead of sticks, and no ice-skates.

number of people – beyond that you have to buy an additional room or pizza. Pizza is harder of course, because you know how many people you can fit in a hotel room, but have no idea how many teens can share a pizza.[19] Order too many pizzas, and you will either run short on money or have leftovers that will probably be tossed. Order too few and you will have hungry teens – which is very bad (hungry teens tend to be uncooperative and easily distracted). Here are some strategies that can help:

- As with group pricing, advance sign-ups with deposits can be very helpful. It is essential for high priced items such as hotel rooms.
- Reserve for the best case (maximum number) turnout, then budget for the worst-case turnout. This will ensure that you have enough for everyone, but won't lose money even if the turnout is bad.
- Keep in mind cancellation rules. You can reserve extra hotel rooms safely if they can be cancelled a few days before the trip.
- Consider setting a maximum attendance. A good example of where this is necessary is bus rentals, where you have a limited number of seats (bus rentals and available cars are a similar problem with regards to budgeting).

Other tips

- If you go to a restaurant with a large group of teens, and have a single bill, it is unlikely that you will collect

---

[19] The highest number of teens per large pizza is about six to eight girls on a diet. Science has not yet discovered the maximum number of pizzas a single teenage boy can devour.

enough money at the first attempt. Even if every teen remembers to pay for everything they ordered, many will not understand how to calculate tax and tip. You can save yourself a great deal of stress, and provide some good leadership training, by teaching one or two of the teens how to do these calculations and put them in charge of collecting the money. Then sit back and relax – it will take a while.

- If the group has a bank account[20], make sure they have a treasurer. Then give them as much freedom as possible in deciding how to spend the money.

---

[20] Currently U.S. regulations generally do not allow minors to be signers on a bank account. If your organization does not have policies regarding bank accounts, you can always open one for them and let them do everything except for signing checks.

Scheduling worksheet

Here's an example of an event outline/schedule:

Event Name: Pizza and Mini-Golf

Goals: A fun evening

Cost per-person or for group: Group discount gives us $3 per-person for golf.

Coordinators/leaders: Jay and Ariel

Meeting time/place: 6:00 pm, Saturday Feb 12 at the community center

Estimated / Max attendance: 20-30. Need at least 10 for the group discount.

Other groups invited: No

Staffing/chaperones: Jay's dad and our group advisor.

Schedule:

Time	What	Where	People	Supplies
6:00pm	Meet, hangout	Community center		
6:30pm	Welcome, announcements	Community center	Group president, others with announcements	Hand out pizza coupons.
6:45pm	Drive to pizza	Address & phone # of pizza place	Event coordinator, Drivers	Printed directions to pizza place
7:00pm	Eat dinner	Pizza place		
8:00pm	Drive to Mini-golf	Address & phone # of mini-golf	Event coordinator	Directions to mini-golf
8:15pm	Split into teams	In front of mini-golf	Event coordinators, team captains	Tournament rules
8:45pm	Tournament starts	Mini-golf	Team captains	
10:00pm	Closing program. Give out awards. Announce next event	Near exit	Event coordinator, team captains. Group president	Flyers for next week's program

43 - Energy levels

The term "energy level" refers to the energy level of the participants at a program. An athletic event or program based on a contest or game would tend to have a very high energy level, with lots of physical activity, excitement, shouting and noise.

An indoor arts or crafts program or one that involves role-playing might be an intermediate energy program.
A discussion program, or watching a film, would tend to be a low energy program.

Teaching teens about energy levels gives them a powerful tool for assembling multiple programs into an event. The key is to understand how the energy level of participants relates to the energy level of the activities they are planning.

You can gradually move from high to low energy activities or vice versa. But you cannot move people back and forth quickly. If people are relaxed from watching a film, you will have a hard time getting them up for a high-energy athletic program. Similarly, it is hard to quiet people down after a high-energy program, (unless it is so high energy that they become exhausted – which is a legitimate programming technique). Try to organize programs so they have a gradual transition – slow to moderate to high, or high to moderate to low. If you try rapid changes – a high-energy program, followed by a low energy program, followed by another high-energy program – there is a good chance your final program will fail. People simply will not cooperate.

Sometimes even the best program will fail because it is designed for one energy level but the group happens to be at another energy level. For example: if everyone is excited and energetic, an attempt to have a quiet and serious discussion might simply fail as the group finds itself unable to sit still and pay attention. Or, if a group is really tired, you may not be able to get them up for a high-energy game no matter how hard you try. There is no perfect way to prevent this from happening – sometimes you just get unlucky. Using a backup plan (if available) or improvising a suitable activity at the last minute may be your only options in this case.

44 - Flexibility

They say no war plan survives its first engagement with the enemy. Few event plans survive engagement with participants. Flexibility is essential – but how do you teach that?

- Encourage planners to consider numerous "what-if" scenarios and consider how they might respond to them.
- Point out areas in the plan where problems might occur – especially timing issues. Teens often underestimate how long it takes to move a group from one place to another, or even how long it takes to get a group quiet.
- When problems occur, help them to respond. By helping, I don't mean solve the problem for them. Rather, point out the positive – that this is a challenge to face, and an opportunity to be flexible, and that you have confidence in their ability to adapt. Help them quickly brainstorm solutions, and challenge them to come to a decision.

Flexibility is not only required when problems occur. Sometimes, if you are very lucky, magic strikes – and a program goes extremely well. If things are on a roll, embrace the moment. Don't just cut it off because the schedule says time is up – see if there are ways to jigger the schedule to let it continue.

For example: our group holds business meetings on weeknights every other week that are supposed to be over by 10pm. Sometimes they have a program called a "good and welfare" at the end of the meeting, where everyone has a chance to talk without interruption. Usually we have a time limit to make sure everyone has a chance to speak. On one particular night, some issues that had been simmering began to come out. People were speaking from the heart, and it was very intense and emotional. Time limits were stretched, and it was clear that people didn't just want to speak, they needed to speak. So I ignored the time limit and we went on until after 11.

The next day I fielded some phone calls from parents and my supervisor, but I stood my ground – and they accepted (with only minor reluctance) my judgment that this was an unusual and important exception to the rule. The experience indeed proved to have great long-term benefits for the group, as members could now talk openly about some problems that needed to be faced and addressed.

Part IV - Topics

There are so many topics that you will face and teach as a youth advisor that it would take a lifetime to cover them all, and even then something will come up that surprises you. I am still constantly astonished by the new situations that come my way.

In this part of the book, we will explore a few of the most important topics that will help you in your role. Some of these are issues that you will face and need to deal with.

Many of the chapters in this section cover subjects that you may want to teach to your teens. In fact, much of the material you will find here has been adapted from programs that I have run or taught over the years – programs that have been proven effective time and again.

45 - Communication skills

If being a role-model and setting an example is the most important leadership skill, there is little doubt that communication skills are a close second. Whether it is speaking in front of a group, talking one on one, chatting online or sending an email or text message, effective communication is an essential part of both what you do as an adult, and what teen leaders will be doing on a daily basis.

The best way to teach these skills is to set an example – but that approach has one big limitation. Though most adults do well in writing or on a one-to-one basis, many have a difficult time with public speaking. In fact, some studies show that public speaking is the most frightening thing people face – second only to death.

If you have good communication skills, use them. Find opportunities to speak to the group on a variety of issues, even if they only indirectly relate to the activities of the group. If you do not have good communication skills, then set an example in trying to improve. If they see you trying to learn and overcome your own limitations, that will give them the confidence to do so as well. Instead of you being the "teacher", you will be learning these skills together – which can be just as effective (and sometimes even more so).

In the sections that follow, you will learn a few key concepts and techniques that you will be able to use even if you yourself are not a skilled communicator[21].

Public speaking

Different organizations offer different opportunities for public speaking. Some have meetings where group leaders or officers have the opportunity to give reports. Teens almost always have a chance to speak to the group at the start of an event and perhaps during activities (even if it's only to get things organized). It is almost always possible to carve out additional opportunities to speak at the start of an activity.

As the adult advisor, you can also use these opportunities to speak to the group and improve your own skills. When doing so, try to focus on topics that do not place you in the position of trying to lead the group. For example: let's say the group is doing a fundraiser for a charitable cause. You might have different teens speaking to advocate for the group that they wish to receive the contribution. Instead of advocating for a group, you might choose to speak briefly on the moral values relating to charitable giving. In doing so, you reinforce the decision of the group to do the fundraiser and perhaps inspire them to do even better – but you are not influencing the immediate decision as to which charity will receive the donation. You are thus leaving the leadership in the hands of the teens and acting in a supportive role.

---

[21] And lest you wonder if I'm qualified to offer advice on this subject, not only have I spoken in front of the youth group on innumerable occasions; I spent over 15 years on the speaker circuit at technical conferences worldwide speaking to groups ranging from a half dozen to several thousand.

Overcoming fear

I can't think of how many times I have heard the most common recommendation for overcoming fear of public speaking – to imagine the audience in their underwear. Frankly, I don't think that would make me (or the typical teenager) any less nervous.

Here's the suggestion I offer people to help them relax in front of a group:

- Stand in front of the group and concentrate first on physically relaxing and smiling.
- Pick out two or three friends (or friendly faces) in the audience – preferably two near the front who are a bit separated, and one a bit farther back in the center.
- Then make eye contact those people only – ignoring everyone else in the room. When you start speaking, speak to them – switching between them every few sentences.

This works for two reasons:

- Because they are your friends, their reactions should be very positive and supportive.
- Because they are a bit spread out, the fact that you are ignoring all but three of the people in the room will not be obvious.

Once you are comfortable with this strategy, it is fairly easy to start making eye contact with more and more people in the room. A few successes and that deep fear of public speaking will ease and be replaced with normal excitement and pre-speech jitters.

Relax, it's just a speech

Many people become very stressed at the idea of giving a "speech". The idea of a formal presentation is intimidating.

When they start writing out the speech they struggle to find the "right" words, to sound intelligent, and to be erudite. Next thing you know, they become incredibly stressed. And when it becomes time to present the speech, they become overwhelmed by the anxiety and collapse into a puddle of sweat[22].

Here's my advice: Relax, it's just a speech.

Don't use highly formal language. Don't get literary.

Write it out as if you were casually talking to a group of friends. If it is an impromptu speech, just stand there and chat with people as if they were a group of friends gathered in your living room.

Emotion and logic

When teaching speaking skills, I tend to focus more on presentation than content. That's because, in my experience, the teens know what they want to say – and if not, they can be helped to develop content with a few well chosen questions.

From a leadership development perspective, it is best to avoid contributing content to a speech. It is their speech, and the last thing you want is for it to become in any way your speech.

Presentation, on the other hand, is an area where you can help a great deal – because all you are doing is helping them to become more effective at communicating their own content. Or put another way – it is not OK to tell them what to say; it is OK to teach them how to say it well.

---

[22] This happened to me the first time I spoke in front of a large audience. Curiously, surviving the nightmare scenario increased my confidence the next time. Since I'd already experienced the worst, I figured my next attempt would have to be better – and it was.

That said, there is one content related issue that you can and should teach the teens. There is a tendency to focus on logic, reason and ideas as they write out their speech. Logic, reason and ideas are very important, but they are not enough – a speech is not the same thing as an essay.

A good speech must have emotional content as well – the emotions carry the ideas. Feelings, passion, inspiration, excitement – these are the tools for conveying ideas and influencing others. These are the tools of leadership.

Consider these two paragraphs from a speech:

- "We should clean up after ourselves at restaurants so that we will be welcomed back on future visits".
- "Last time we ate out we left a mess. What are we? Pigs? Are we going to be like those slacker teens that people look at with disgust? NO! We're better than that! We're going to be the group that is welcomed back everywhere we go because of the way we clean up after ourselves."

The first example is a nice logical argument that will likely be ignored. The second one is an impassioned speech that will likely cause a change in the behavior of the group. They make the same argument and contain the same ideas; but in the second example, the emotional content carries the idea.

Teaching Techniques

There are a great many techniques for teaching speech. Ultimately, the only way to learn to speak in front of others is to do it. One of the best ways is through a speech workshop, where you invite teens to speak on a subject and then critique them (or better, have the entire group critique them). You can also videotape speakers and show them what they look like. When doing a workshop of this kind, here are some things to watch for and to try.

- Remind participants to frame their criticism as positive-negative-positive.
- Consider showing some video examples of great speakers. Point out what makes them great (see things to look for below). Some of my favorites (that you can find online) include:
  - Kenneth Branagh's speech before the battle of Agincourt from Henry V.
  - Martin Sheen's speeches in the West Wing episodes " 20 Hours in America" and "College Kids".
  - President Barak Obama's Nobel Acceptance speech.
  - President John F. Kennedy's Inaugural Address.
  - Dr. Martin Luther King Jr.'s "I Have a Dream" speech.
  - President Ronald Reagan's "Tear Down This Wall " speech in Berlin.
- Listen for tone. Help monotone speakers to vary their voice.
- Look for stance. Speakers who exhibit rocking or repetitive motion should be taught to be more still or deliberate in their motion. Speakers who are frozen in place should be helped to walk as they speak.
- Look for hand motions. You are looking for natural gestures – not hands in pockets.

- Look for energy. Good speakers project energy forward towards the audience (lean forward or step forward, and make eye contact)
- Watch for speakers who laugh at themselves during a speech. This indicates a lack of confidence. They are laughing at themselves preemptively because of fear that others will laugh at them.
- Use emotions and styles to correct problems. For example: Have a very quiet speaker repeat their speech angrily, or yelling. Have a loud speaker whisper theirs.
- Try karaoke to build confidence standing in front of a group.
- Teach them that speech is a performance art – how you present is as important as the content.
- Don't be afraid to try different things and to push the teens to try different things. If one approach doesn't work, try something else.

Public speaking is a skill that can be learned. Once you help someone overcome the fear of speaking, you will be amazed how quickly they can improve. I have seen very poor speakers deliver remarkable presentations after just 10-15 minutes of training.

Attention and focus

Before you can start speaking, you need to get people's attention – and that is a skill in and of itself.

The most important concept to understand in this regard is that of "the focus" – the idea that everyone in the group has their attention focused on the speaker. As long as you have the focus, you can speak and people will listen (or at least pretend to listen). If you drop the focus, it doesn't matter what you say – people will be paying attention to something else or talking among themselves.

Here is an ideal example of how things might work at the start of an event when several teens want to make announcements:

- Leaders spread themselves throughout the room to help get people quiet
- On the first speaker's signal, the leaders get the people around them quiet without speaking – just a whisper or tap on the shoulder should be enough. They also turn their attention to the first speaker – setting an example for those near them to follow.
- As soon as it is quiet, the first speaker starts – speaking clearly and concisely.
- As soon as the first speaker is finished, they pass the focus to the next speaker. This is typically done with a statement and gesture. For example: saying "And now, Michelle has an announcement about the upcoming community service event" while pointing to Michelle and looking at her. This directs the focus of the group to Michelle.
- This kind of focus hand-off continues until everyone has spoken.

Here are some of the techniques you and your teens should use:

- Don't speak until it is quiet and you have the focus. Give the techniques you learned in Chapter 39 (Principles of leadership) a chance to work.
- Start speaking the instant it is quiet or perhaps an instant before.

- Stay focused on what you are saying. Don't let anyone distract you. If you turn around to talk to someone else, you will drop the focus and have to work again to regain it.
- Be prepared. Know what you are going to say. You owe that to your audience. Don't waste their time. Don't ramble. Once you've made your point, pass the focus (or move on to the next item on the agenda).
- Remember to hand-off the focus to the next speaker. You can ping-pong focus between two people as long as each one is careful to pass the focus back to the other.
- If someone interrupts (steals the focus), respond firmly and grab the focus back. For example: you're talking about a fundraiser and someone interrupts with a joke. Everyone laughs. You respond loudly "That's hysterical, but what won't be funny is if we don't raise $100 next week..."

These techniques are simple enough to understand, but surprisingly hard to follow. Don't be surprised if you have to teach these techniques many times, and illustrate them with many examples, before you begin to see results.

Writing

When you think about leadership, most of the time you think about verbal communication (whether speaking in front of a group or one-on-one). But it's important not to forget about written communication.

Written communication, whether it takes the form of email, text messages, chat or articles, has several advantages over verbal communication:

- Comprehension. Studies show that written communication results in a higher degree of comprehension and is less likely to be misunderstood than verbal communication. Encourage teens to use written handouts and instructions as part of programs instead of relying solely on spoken instructions.
- Conflict resolution. When in an argument, it is common to start formulating a response while the other person is still speaking. The need to respond quickly reduces the time for thought and deliberation. While writing can be just as inflammatory as speech (see any online flame war), it does slow down communication enough to allow for additional reflection.
- Power and permanence. When you write an email to a teen (as compared to calling or speaking in person), the message carries additional weight. At the very least, it shows that you have put a great deal of thought into the issue, and taken the trouble to write it out. Criticism (presented, as always, in a positive-negative-positive form) often works best in email. A compliment carries more weight in writing. If you really want to blow someone away – mail them a letter. Despite (or because of) today's advanced technology, an old-fashioned written letter can have an enormous impact.

46 - Sex, drugs, and rock & roll

At some point in your time as a youth advisor, you are going to have to deal with all three of these issues. Of them, the only one that is easy is rock & roll. Forget the stereotype that as an adult you won't like their music. These days, odds are almost certain that you can find some musical common ground with every teen you meet.

But be sure you always have some nice relaxing music on hand. Because you'll need it whenever the other two issues in this chapter come up.

Sex

Every youth organization deals with sex in different ways. Some promote abstinence to such a degree that they don't even acknowledge an alternative exists. Some host conventions with so much behind the scenes sexual activity the staff is grateful when the teens don't go home pregnant. Some groups openly accept gay teens, others expel them. Perhaps no subject is more complex and sensitive.

I won't even begin to try to advocate a particular approach – it's not my job here to promote a specific set of values. That said, there are certain universal principles that apply to any group.

- Find out your organization's viewpoint before you open your mouth on the topic. If you say something contrary to the official view of the organization, there's a fair chance you'll be invited to leave (especially if a parent complains about something you said). It's not that this is a more important topic than any of the others, it's just more sensitive.[23]

- Regardless of your organization's view on teen sexuality, the teens in your group will be thinking about, talking about, and more than likely participating in some sort of sexual activity. Only people who have no memory of being a teenager think otherwise.

- In most groups, sex education is not a part of your job. If your organization allows you to answer questions on sex, only do so if you feel comfortable answering and if you are sure you have correct information. Otherwise, pass any questions up to your supervisor.

- Do not share stories of your own sex life with the teens. It is none of their business. Do not ask them about their sex lives. It is none of your business (and may well be illegal).

- Do not ever, under any circumstances, regardless of provocation, have any sort of sexual contact with the teens you work with (even if the teen is old enough, or you are close enough in age so that it may be legal in your state).

Drugs and alcohol

Drugs and alcohol are simpler to deal with than sex since virtually every youth group today takes a similar stand – that both drugs and alcohol are bad, and that any teen that shows up at an event drunk or high should be sent home and experience appropriate consequences.

---

[23] Here sensitive means: a topic on which some parents tend to go completely nuts.

With teen drug use as prevalent as it is today, a simple zero-tolerance policy that punishes individuals who use drugs is not enough. You and the group can be instrumental in preventing drug use by creating a culture that discourages it.

Here are some facts and techniques you can use to help create that kind of culture:

- Not everyone agrees on the danger of drugs, particularly pot. Many will argue that marijuana is less harmful than tobacco or alcohol. But what everyone agrees on is that any substance is more dangerous to kids and teens than to adults. In more than 20 years as an advisor, I have seen very few individuals run into serious trouble with pot if they started in college. No teen, that I have seen, that started at 13 or 14 got by unscathed.

- The impact of drugs and alcohol depends very much on the individual. Some can use substances recreationally with little harm, others become alcoholics or addicts or worse. So introducing another teen to drugs or alcohol is like playing Russian roulette – you don't know what degree of harm you might do. This is an important message for older teens.[24] They should not assume, based on their own experience, how these substances might impact someone else. And they might unintentionally ruin someone's life.

- Drug use and drinking by members of a group can harm the reputation of the group, even if it takes place outside of official group activities. Parents care (rightly) about who their teens are associating with.

---

[24] You'll probably have to explain Russian roulette to them as well. Look it up online if you don't know the reference.

Any group that gets a reputation for drinking and drug use will have a difficult time recruiting, or obtaining parental or community support.

All of these facts can and should be shared with your group. You see, many teens are taught about the "evils" of drugs and drinking in a very absolute manner. They leave those lessons with the idea that even one drink or smoke can destroy their life.

Unfortunately and inevitably, the day arrives where they see a friend experiment (or experiment themselves) and find, somewhat to their surprise, that their life is not immediately ruined. At which point they conclude that all of the anti-drug messages were a lie and that they can safely continue drinking or smoking.

That is the nature of substance abuse – by the time it actually hurts you, it is very hard to stop. What's more, the person abusing the substances denies that any harm is occurring. Their grades can drop, relations with parents can go bad, they can even lose their friends, and they will still blame everything but the substances.

If you present a consistent and fact based anti-drug message, you may, if you are very lucky, delay experimentation with substances by teens in your group. By stressing to the teen leaders the potential impact that they have as role models to younger members, you may be able to get the leaders to delay or stop substance use – or at the very least convince them to be discrete and not share or introduce it to younger members.

But no matter what you do, some of the teens you work with will get involved with drugs or alcohol – and all of the problems that come with that. Don't take it personally, and be grateful for the successes you have.

It also goes without saying that you should never provide any drugs or alcohol to any teens. Nor should you be present at any occasion or location where drug or alcohol use by members of your group is occurring. What does this mean in practice? If you are throwing a party where drugs or alcohol may be present, do not invite any of the teens. If you find yourself at a social event where teens, and drugs or alcohol are present – leave.

Tobacco and Caffeine

These are drugs too. The only difference is that they are legal and accepted in our society. Twenty years ago when I started as a youth group advisor, smoking was allowed in our organization. About 16 years ago it was banned, curiously enough by the teens themselves.[25] Today tobacco use and standards vary by location and organization, but is generally discouraged everywhere.

Caffeine continues to be legal of course, and very popular. But that doesn't mean you should ignore it completely. I have one member in the group right now who is banned from drinking caffeinated energy drinks at events ever since the evening I found him shaking uncontrollably after drinking one.

---

[25] This was partly because the majority did not like smoking, and partly because the regional president at the time was a smoker. Banning smoking was a way for the membership to show their disapproval of the way he was doing his job. The ban on smoking was then incorporated into the region's policies.

47 - Driving

If you are working with teens, depending on where you are located and the policies of your organization, you may be dealing with teen drivers. For parents, of course, this is almost inevitable. The organization I work with allows teens to drive at events (which is almost a necessity here in California, where public transit is very limited and everything is very spread out). As such, I've worked with hundreds of teen drivers; and I have some good news and some bad news.

The good news is that in all over 20 years, none of our teens has suffered more than a minor injury due to a car accident.

The bad news is that everything else you have heard about teen drivers is more or less true. I would say that most of our drivers have gotten into at least one fender bender or close call. It is a rare teen driver that I haven't had to at least once come up and talk to about safe driving. One of our teen drivers was so dangerous that the group itself voted to ban him from driving other teens at events.

Here is one example that I find illustrative. One evening two of our drivers were goofing off in an empty parking lot – driving slowly around in circles. There we were: two cars, a large empty parking lot, the rest of the group watching at the side, and me yelling at them to park. You can guess what happened next. Somehow, despite the all the space they had available, the two cars found each other. The cars were totaled. The drivers were uninjured, but very embarrassed. Their parents were not happy.

I have a handout that I give to new drivers. You can find a version of it in Appendix A of this book. When you read it, look beyond the facts (which are obvious) to the tone that I used. The emphasis is on responsibilities, expectations and rights – not warnings or threats.

48 - Bad kids and troubled teens

Father O'Malley, in the movie *"Boy's Town"* said, "There is no such thing as a bad boy". I wish I could agree with that statement. I might agree that nobody is born "bad", but by the time they grow to be teens there are, I am afraid, some who are truly lost, some who are morally bankrupt, some who are self-destructive, and some who carelessly destroy others.

The good news is these are few and far between. Most teens, like most people in general, are basically good - flawed and prone to mistakes, but decent nonetheless.

Unfortunately, society is much more willing to label and discard teens than most people realize. From zero-tolerance policies that lead to huge consequences for honest mistakes, to over diagnosis of ADD and ADHD, to a general degree of suspicion on the part of teachers and other adults – it is tough to be a teen. And it is not hard to get slapped with a label such as "troublemaker" or "disrespectful" or "uncooperative".

Once a teen gets labeled in this manner, it becomes hard to break out of it. At school, classes are large. It is a lot easier to send a kid to the principal than try to resolve their issues. And it is more fun as a teacher to spend time with the "good" kids than struggle with the "bad" ones.

For some of these teens, a youth group may be their best opportunity to be successful – not just as a teen but as an adult as well.

I'm not going to tell you to reach out to these teens and try to convince them to be cooperative and constructive members of the group. That will likely fail. What you really need to consider is putting them in charge. Give them as much responsibility as you possibly can as quickly as you can.

There is an old story I read as a child about a group of sailors in a lifeboat who had a limited amount of water. The officer was the only one with a gun, and was using it to control the crew and make sure the water rationing was strictly followed. Finally, too exhausted to stay awake, he handed the gun to his bo'sun (the lead crewman, and the one who was most eager to distribute the water right away) and told him to handle things. Then he fell asleep, knowing that he had failed. He woke up to find the bo'sun offering him his water ration. Surprised that there was any water left, he asked what happened. The bo'sun explained that he had been ready to kill for the water; but when he had control over the boat, everything changed and he felt responsible for everyone. The bo'sun continued the rationing and, as a result, everyone ultimately survived.

Responsibility is a very powerful thing – especially for teens (who sometimes do not get it, or the respect that comes with it, in school or at home).

Whether as a teacher or as a youth advisor, when I see a teen who is acting out or talking back, I try to find a way to put them in charge of something as quickly as possible. It does not always work, but I've found nothing that works better.

Troubled teens

There's that old cliché – don't judge someone until you've walked a mile in their shoes. The teens you work with each come with their own baggage. Problems at home or school will spill over to other aspects of their lives. Problems with relationships (and when you're a teen, any relationship is, almost by definition, a problem), will impact everything in their life.

You won't always know what is going on in their lives outside of events. But you may find that you know more than any other adult (including their parents). Some of them will come to you for advice. For serious issues, refer to Chapter 51 on "Dealing with crisis". In general, the best thing you can do is listen – it is not your job to solve their problems (nor are you likely to be able to, even if you wanted to). But lending a sympathetic ear is valuable and important.

Here are some of the issues that you are likely to see. Remember, don't hesitate to ask for help dealing with any of these.

School Issues

School is one of the major factors in the life of any teen. Aside from being one of their primary sources of knowledge and information, it is without doubt one of their primary sources of stress. Competition for even mid-level colleges has increased tremendously. Aside from encouraging teens to get a good education, and listening sympathetically to their stories, there are a few other things you can do to help them out:

- Encourage them to get enough sleep. Many teens don't sleep enough, making it harder for them to concentrate (or even stay awake) at school and magnifying the impact of stress.
- Teaching time management techniques (as described in Chapter 52) can be very helpful to teens in school, as well as with their youth group activities.
- At some point you may be asked to write a letter of recommendation. I encourage you to do so if you can;

or answer with a polite "I don't think I'm the right person to do this" if you feel that you really aren't the right person for that particular recommendation (or in the unlikely event that you are asked to write a letter by someone for whom you can't honestly write a good recommendation).

- Remind you seniors that their life does not end if they don't get into the school of their choice. There are many paths to success, and going directly to a four year college is only one of them.

Family or personal crisis

Depending on the size of your group, you are likely at some point to have teens in your group that face a serious family crisis: divorce, illness, job loss and so forth. In my group I typically see a few of these every year. The most common one I've seen for teens is the death of a grandparent. Job loss varies depending on the economy. I've also dealt with teens who themselves were seriously ill, or whose parents were seriously ill – even a case where a parent committed suicide. The principles for dealing with all of these issues are roughly the same:

- Be there. Reach out if not asked. Listen or respond if approached. This may include a hospital visit or even attending a funeral. It may involve just listening or responding to emails or text messages.
- Teach the rest of the group how to respond. If you feel you don't know what to say, it's a safe bet the other teens have no idea how to respond. Discuss the situation and help them see how they can support their friend. Their response is generally more important than yours.

- Provide resources. You might be able to help track down counseling resources (in a family crisis the parents may be too occupied to do so). You might be able to track down scholarship opportunities for special programs or other activities after a parent loses their job.
- It's OK to say "I'm sorry, I don't know what to say" or "I wish I had the words to make you feel better." Avoid telling stories of bad things that happened to you or saying that things will get better with time. Neither help at the moment of crisis (though they may be appropriate later). The single best thing you can do is to be there and listen if the teen wants to talk. Just sitting there in silence can be enough.

Depression and Mental Illness

The teen years are years of incredibly rapid growth and change. Those changes apply to the brain as well – which is why mental changes and depression often manifest at this age. Unless you happen to be a trained psychologist, don't try to diagnose the teens you work with. Remember that one of the consequences of all those raging hormones is moodiness – so don't be surprised if your teens go through periods of sadness, exuberance, detachment and engagement (and everything in between). But if, after knowing them for a while, something feels "off", trust your instincts and bring your concerns to your supervisor.

Be aware that teens don't always try drugs due to peer pressure or curiosity. Sometimes they are, in effect, self-medicating for depression.

Depression and mental illness require professional help. In either of these cases either you or your supervisor should contact the parents. If you are lucky, the parents will respond to your observations and will seek out the appropriate help. Don't be surprised if their reaction is denial that any problem exists.

Abuse, Suicide and Violence

The good news is that in most communities these are not nearly as common as the other issues listed in this chapter. How to handle them is covered in the next chapter.

49 - Confidentiality

You might think that sex and drugs are the toughest issues you will deal with when working with teens. But compared to confidentiality, they are a piece of cake.

The crux of the problem is simple:

As a youth advisor, if you are even halfway decent, you will come to know things about your teens that their parents are not aware of. Things that you would certainly want to know about your teen if you were (or are) a parent. You will know which teens are sexually active, drinking, doing drugs, driving dangerously, stealing from their employers, or running porn sites on their dad's computer[26].

If you report everything you hear or see to parents, the teens will quickly see you as a spy. They will not trust you and you will not be able to act effectively. Given that one of the roles of a youth advisor in most organizations is to be an adult that teens in the group can approach who isn't their parent, it's clear that interpreting your role as being a spy for the parents is probably not a good idea.

At the same time, there are going to be issues that you cannot and should not keep confidential. So what do you do?

Let's start at the beginning...

Find out if you are a mandated reporter

A mandated reporter is an individual who is legally obligated to report certain types of abuse to their local child protective services department. Mandated reporter laws spell out exactly what needs to be reported and how to report it.

---

[26] I wish I could say that these are hypothetical examples. They are not.

A mandated reporter can be prosecuted for failing to report abuse and cannot be held liable for an erroneous report that is made in good faith.

Mandated reporter laws vary from state to state and can be quite complex. For example: in California, if you are a paid staff member for a youth organization, you are likely to be a mandated reporter, but if you are a volunteer, you typically are not.

It is important to distinguish between your organization's policies and your legal requirements. For example: a youth organization in California might require its volunteers to report suspected abuse, but they cannot make them mandated reporters. The difference? If you aren't a mandated reporter and fail to make a report, the worst they can do to you is fire you. If you are, you can be prosecuted by the state.

Depending on the organization, you may have other legal requirements with regards to confidentiality. Court Appointed Special Advocates (CASA) for example, are subject to numerous legal requirements that they protect the confidentiality of the foster kids they work with.

It is your organization's responsibility to inform you of your legal requirements. But I encourage you to do your own research as well, because some organizations either do not make the effort or they get it wrong. In particular, national organizations may not be aware of state laws that apply to you.

Find out your organization's policies with regards to confidentiality

Don't be surprised if some of those policies are vague or don't make much sense. This is not a simple topic and there are rarely easy answers. If an organization's policies were written up by lawyers, they will be written to protect the organization from being sued – which isn't necessarily what is best for the teens. In fact, the vaguer the policies, the more likely they were written by some very smart and experienced people who have figured out that trusting their advisors' judgment is a sound strategy.

An organization's philosophy and goals will have a great impact on how they view confidentiality and a good organization will communicate those values to you. Most organizations appreciate the importance of confidentiality, and will help you learn to make judgments that are best for the teens and are compatible with the organization's values.

The imminent danger standard

There are some confidentiality decisions that are easy. If you feel a teen is in imminent danger you should tell someone. What does imminent danger mean? It means that you believe that they are at high risk of being hurt, or hurting themselves or others in the immediate future. If a teen says something that leads to you think they may go home and commit suicide, or show up at school the next day with a gun to kill someone, don't sit on it – tell someone![27] Your organization should have procedures in place for you to follow in these kinds of situations.

Don't be afraid to talk to the teen about these issues. Talking about suicide will not increase the chances of a teen trying it.

Be open about confidentiality issues

To break a confidence that you have promised to keep is one of the worst things you can do working with teens. So it is very important that you not promise to keep confidential things that you can't.

If you are a mandated reporter, you should absolutely explain to the teens what that means and let them know that you will not keep confidence if those kinds of issues come up. The teens I work with know that I will not keep confidence if I feel someone is in imminent danger.

Does letting them know you won't keep confidence on these issues mean you are less likely to hear about them? In some cases yes – though in others they may tell you anyway as a way of asking for help. But remember – your role is not to be a spy, it's to be an advisor, a counselor and a friend.

If you must break confidence, if at all possible let the teen know first. Explain why you must do so. It's not ideal, but it's better than them finding out later from someone else that you betrayed them.

---

[27] I've thankfully never had to address the issue of a teen bringing a gun to school, though I did once have to explain to a teen that bringing a machete to a youth group event was a very bad idea. Unfortunately, I cannot say the same about potential suicides. I've dealt with too many of those – none of which, thankfully, have been completed.

And if you accidentally break a confidence and let something slip that you shouldn't have, apologize quickly and profusely. You will likely be forgiven – teens understand that secrets sometimes slip out by accident.

50 - Playing favorites

I know what you're thinking – you should never play favorites, right?

Wrong.

First of all, you are human. This means that there will be some teens you click with, and others that rub you the wrong way. There will be some teens who like you, and some who don't. So you're going to have favorites.

But more important, there will also be some teens who simply want or need more of your time than others, either because they have more to learn and need more help, because they need help dealing with issues in their lives, or because they are genuinely interested in learning from you or hearing your perspective. Also, there will be some teens who are natural leaders who you will tend to work with more. There will be others who have leadership potential that are worth the investment of some extra time. If you are working to develop youth leadership, you will naturally spend the bulk of your time with the youth leaders and potential leaders – helping and teaching them to work with the group as a whole.

So you won't be treating all of the members equally.

What is important, however, is that you are fair... that you give everyone equal opportunity to succeed. You should offer your time and energy to any of the teens who wish to take you up on that offer.

Or put another way – it's OK to play favorites as long as you're not the one choosing who the favorites are. Allow the teens to determine for themselves to what degree, and in what manner, to use you as a resource.

51 - Dealing with crisis

Being a youth advisor is scary. After all, you are responsible for the health and safety of a group of teens. In a program where you are encouraging youth leadership, it is even scarier – because they are making decisions, but you (as the adult) remain responsible for what takes place. That's why even after the teens have taken on a leadership role, you still have to pay attention to what is going on. Because sooner or later, a crisis will hit.

Preparing the teens

Part of crisis preparation involves working with the teens to define your role in the context of teen leadership. This will vary depending on the nature of the group. My approach is to make it clear and explicit that even though they have complete control over all of the group's decisions and activities (as long as they are within the rules of the organization), in the event of an emergency (as defined by me), I expect them to listen and follow my instructions immediately and without question. I also explain to them the importance of bringing to my attention any issues relating to health and safety.

For example:

At one event a younger teen was having a hypoglycemic attack. One of the teen leaders noticed he was looking ill and was told by the youngster that he needed a candy bar. The teen leader (who was pretty smart, and also didn't have a candy bar on hand) brought this to my attention. My immediate response was to have him call everyone together (interrupting the program that was going on) to find out if anyone had some candy. Since nobody had any, I directed one of the older teens to go to a nearby store and get some right away. This is, of course, a relatively minor emergency. The teen having the attack knew what was going on and what needed to be done. Since it was a health issue, I did not hesitate to interrupt the activity and tell the teens what I needed to have happen right away.

All of the teens I've worked with, no matter how independent, have felt that this is a reasonable arrangement. Because I respected their authority over the group, they have been willing to respect my authority over matters of health and safety and interpretation of the organization's rules. Again I stress that this arrangement is explicit. It is something we discuss once or twice a year so that even the newest members understand their responsibilities, as well as my own.

Preparing yourself

There isn't a great deal you can do to prepare for the unexpected; but you can expect certain problems to come up and prepare for them.

- You should have emergency contact information for your supervisor (and a backup number), so you can contact someone in the organization for help if necessary. Most organizations will also have a mechanism for reporting certain kinds of incidents after they happen – so prepare to take notes afterwards so that you can report what occurred.
- Buy a nice size first-aid kit and know how to use it. Keep it in your car. You WILL use it.
- Know your organization's policies regarding dispensing medication. Personally, I won't even give a teen under 18 an aspirin without authorization from a parent.

- Generally speaking, teens are old enough to be responsible for managing their own medical conditions (such as knowing not to eat food they are allergic to). For younger kids you should be aware of significant medical issues. In the past, it was common for youth group advisors to carry medical releases containing medical and insurance information – especially on campouts and trips. Under today's medical privacy laws this is not always the case. Your organization should be able to provide you with guidelines.
- For any events that are not local, you should have the cell phone numbers of every teen traveling with you. For campouts and overnight trips, you should have contact information for all the parents as well as a release form provided by the organization. If they don't have a release form, you can find examples online (search for "Child care authorization" and you'll find numerous examples, including sites that will create forms for you based on your needs).

Emergencies

Most of the emergencies you are likely to face will be medical. I've sat in emergency rooms with teens for everything from tick bites, to cuts, to broken bones, to second degree sunburns. Regardless of the nature of the emergency, the teens will be looking to you for guidance. The following guidelines will help:

- Stay calm. If you panic, so will the teens.
- Assess the situation. What has to be done immediately, and what can wait.

- Act. Give the teens clear instructions as to what you need them to do.

Yes, I know these are vague; but that is the nature of an emergency – each one is different. Trust yourself. You'll do fine.

Other crisis

As a trusted adult, teens will turn to you when they are in crisis, whether it is a problem with school, peers or parents.

It is not your job to solve the crisis. Not that you shouldn't be supportive, or offer help and advice. I say this to stress that their crisis is not your crisis, and that your ability to fix the situation will usually be quite limited.

There are three main ways that you can help.

- Remain calm and objective. It's a safe bet that the teen will be in a very emotional state. It's up to you to be a calming influence.
- Listen. Believe me, teens have plenty of people ready to tell them what they should do or must do. Having someone who listens is not as common. Listen to what they say. Ask questions. Be sympathetic. And be honest.
- Offer resources. Your community probably has many organizations available to help teens in trouble – know how to find them (search online or use local listings). Services in many areas are offered at the county or city level. Check your county or city web site for more information. Your local phone book may also have resources in the first section of the book. In my time as an advisor, I've given out numbers for adolescent drug treatment programs, counseling centers,

teen crisis hotlines, suicide hotlines, and planned parenthood centers (and have researched similar resources for parents as well). Your supervisor should also be able to serve as a source for advice and resources.

52 - Life skills

One of the goals of any youth group is to teach life skills, and among the most important assets that any advisor brings to a group are their own life skills. One of the very first examples of this I encountered was when I had to teach the chapter treasurer how to balance a checkbook.

The trick with life skills is not to come up with a list of things that you want to teach, but rather to wait until the need appears. Once you see the need, you can talk it over with the teens to find out if they also see the need. If they do, offer to do some training. Don't worry if you do not know how to teach the subject – in most cases all you need to do is a bit of research on the Internet and you'll find plenty of material you can use.

Here's an example:

Our group holds elections every six months, and one of our teens (who I thought had been doing well in the group) lost by a landslide. He came up to me quite upset – wondering what he had been doing wrong. I had no idea.

So I asked him for permission to ask around and see if I could find out what people might have been thinking.

I then spoke with a number of the older members, and got an earful. It turned out that this individual had a very abrasive and even aggressive style. I had not noticed it partly because he did not act that way towards adults, and partly because I simply missed it.

I realized that what he needed was some assertiveness training. Most people think of assertiveness training in the context of helping passive individuals to stand up for themselves. But it can be equally useful in helping aggressive individuals to find ways to accomplish their goals without repelling or offending others. I was able to find a variety of exercises, techniques, and other material for the workshop on the Internet.

Assertiveness training is best taught with a group; and it is certainly a good thing for any teen to learn. So I hosted a workshop open to any teen in the group – encouraging all to attend. As far as everyone was concerned, it was for the benefit of the whole chapter (which it was), but it was also designed specifically to help this one individual.

Any teacher will tell you that there is nothing like teaching people who want to learn – and the workshop was a great success. The teen in question was very highly motivated to learn, and he picked up the concepts quickly. Over the next few months, I kept an eye on him and offered additional feedback. The next time he ran for an office, he won. He ultimately ended up as chapter president, and one of the most respected teens in the group.

Here are some of the most common life skills you may find yourself teaching (aside from the communication skills discussed earlier).

Perseverance

Most of the ideas that teens come up with will never come to fruition. I suppose this is true for adults as well.

The work in any group is never spread out equally. Every successful group has a few individuals who carry most of the load – they have the ability to get things done. In fact, one of the big differences between a successful group and a failed group is the presence of these individuals. In a failing group, nobody steps up to do anything.

As part of leadership training, I discuss this truth – and challenge everyone to step up. I point out that if they choose to become one of those individuals who has the ability to bring ideas into reality, that skill will carry on through their entire life. When speaking with individuals, I often express my confidence that they can become one of those people. Sometimes just having an adult express that kind of faith is enough to make a difference.

Then I point out the "secret" to becoming one of these amazing people who can do anything they want. I explain how most people, when faced with a challenge, stop at the "first excuse". As soon as they have a good legitimate reason to quit, they stop.

For example: a teen wants to plan a dance and tells everyone her great ideas. She decides that she wants to hold it at a local community center. Several weeks go by, and you ask: "by the way, what's up with that dance?" The response: "I tried calling the community center and left messages, but nobody returned my calls."

She had her first excuse – a credible reason to give up that anyone would feel is reasonable and understandable. The result – no dance.

The successful teen would have kept calling, checked the Internet, gone to the community center in person, asked their parents to help contact the community center, asked the advisor to call the community center, explored alternate sites for the dance, and refused to give up.

When a teen stops with the first excuse, call them on it. That doesn't mean do the work for them, or force them to keep trying (both of which involve you taking over the leadership role). It just means letting them know that you think they stopped on the first excuse. It may not make a difference right away; but the next time, they might try a bit harder.

Time management

Some teens have a tendency to over-commit. Others don't come close to undertaking what they are capable of. Few of them have good time management skills. (To be fair, most adults aren't very strong on time management either).

As members of your group become stronger leaders, and try to accomplish more, they will need to improve their time management skills.

Sometimes it's just a matter of helping them to see where they are wasting time. Having them keep a diary for a few days, in which they record what they are doing every 15 minutes, can be a great tool for identifying wasted time.

Sometimes it's a matter of helping them set priorities. Make no mistake – between school, sports, youth group activities, hobbies and extracurricular activities – today's teens can quickly get in over their heads and face some extremely difficult decisions.

What you can do is lay out alternatives, and challenge them to prioritize and perhaps list the advantages and disadvantages of each choice. You might be able to help them identify activities that can be deferred for a while.

Here are a few other points to consider with regards to time management:

- Teens need time for friends, socializing and just hanging out. They even need time to just lie around doing nothing, daydreaming or listening to music. These are not a waste of time, and be sure to encourage them to make these a priority in their lives.

- Many teens do not get enough sleep. Encourage them to make this a priority as well. Do not be surprised if they ignore this advice.
- You'll probably hear complaints about pressure from parents. This can place you in an awkward situation – especially if you know the parents. It's important to be honest about your views, and it is legitimate to offer advice to teens on how they can communicate their views to their parents.
- Never tell the teens what they should choose – even if you are sure you know what is best. You can share your opinion, but always stress to them that it's their decision and you'll respect whatever decision they make – even if their decision is to cut back on youth group activities.

Overcoming fear

Many teens spend a lot of time being afraid. Afraid of failure. Afraid of what others will think. Afraid of not fitting in. Afraid of not being normal. Afraid of not doing well in school. Afraid of disappointing their parents. Afraid of disappointing you. AFRAID THEY ARE THE ONLY ONE WHO FEELS THAT WAY!

Overcoming these fears is one of the greatest challenges they face, and it's one where you can help a great deal.

A good first step is to acknowledge these fears – to help them realize that everyone has these fears to some degree at some times. Here are several good techniques for doing this:

- Talk about fear. Never say "you feel these fears" or "teens are afraid of". Always phrase it "we are afraid of". Always include yourself (and be honest, we adults feel these fears). Talk about examples where you have overcome a fear. This is a good place to set an example.

- Most groups have traditions that allow teens to share their feelings openly. Ours is called "good and welfare". Everyone has a turn to speak without interruption on any subject, and nothing that is said can leave the room. If you remain in the room, be sure the group knows ahead of time your limits in terms of confidentiality. Respect a request to step out if asked, or offer to step out if you feel it more appropriate.

- Various programs exist to share fears. In one, every member anonymously writes down their greatest fear on a piece of paper and drops it in a bag. The program leader then pulls the fears out one at a time and reads them aloud. Be aware: this can be a very intense program and may bring existing crisis situations to your attention.[28]

Beyond acknowledging the fear, probably the best thing you can do is continue to express confidence and faith in their ability to overcome their challenges.

Managing stress

I don't know if teens today are under more stress than I was as a teen – those years are inherently stressful for most

---

[28] One of the most challenging moments I ever had as an advisor was during this type of program. The program leader brought me one of the slips of paper, and I had to interrupt the program, talk on an impromptu basis about suicide, and ask the person who wrote the note that he planned to kill himself to please come and speak to me when the program was over.

of us. But there is no doubt that many teens today experience a great deal of stress, mostly relating to school and parents.

There are many stress management techniques (and many books that focus exclusively on the subject), but when it comes to helping teens cope with stress, focus on the big three:

- Get enough sleep. As mentioned earlier, many teens live in a constant state of sleep deprivation.
- Improve your diet – less junk food, more fruits and vegetables.
- Get some exercise.

It is good advice for them, and odds are you could benefit from following it as well (I know I could).

Procrastination

Sorry, I didn't get this section done in time for this edition.[29]

---

[29] In all seriousness, I have not yet found a way to reliably teach anyone how to stop procrastinating.

53 - Working as a team

Depending on your particular situation, you might be working as part of a team. While it is true that teachers tend to work alone (one per classroom); and parents as pairs or individuals (depending on the family), as an advisor you may be working alone, with a partner, or as part of a team.

While it's often very nice to have a second person around, it always adds complexity to the job and opens the door to a whole set of potential problems and conflicts (as any parent knows). How you manage these potential challenges will have a large impact on both your effectiveness as a team, and your enjoyment as you work with the teens.

Teamwork is a huge subject on which entire books have been written. For now, here are a handful of key principles to keep in mind. I'll use the term "co-advisor" here, but the principles apply to co-teachers and, of course, parents as well.

- Accept the fact that some teens will connect better with one advisor, other teens with the other. This is the main reason why it's good to have more than one advisor in a group – it dramatically increases the chances that every teen will have one adult they are comfortable talking to.

- Unless it is a matter of life and death, never, never, never contradict your co-advisor in front of the teens. You can elaborate on what they are saying if you have something to add. You can ask a question if you feel something needs further clarification. You can take an opposing viewpoint on a debate if the topic is not related to your position (for example: you don't have to agree on world affairs or politics, but you can't contradict a safety or rules decision).

If you disagree with your co-advisor, find a way to discuss it in private. Then, if the decision must be reversed, allow your co-advisor to do so – it is infinitely preferable for an advisor to change their mind, than to be overruled. This especially applies if there is a difference in status or authority. The "senior" advisor should never override the "junior" advisor in public – even if they have the authority to do so. This also applies to supervisors overruling a group advisor.

- Different advisors will have different standards on various issues. The teens should understand and respect that it's possible that one advisor might interpret rules differently or have different safety standards than the other. So when only one of the advisors is present, the group must respect that advisor's standards. When the advisors are together, they should discuss and agree on the standards they will set (with regards to safety standards, you should generally go with the tighter safety standard). Do not let the teens play you off each other.

- Discuss roles. There are infinite ways to divide up responsibilities as an advisor. Talk it over. The last thing you want is a turf battle among the advisors.

- Communicate! Discuss major decisions with your co-advisor beforehand. Brief your co-advisor on any decisions or observations you made so they remain current with what is going on in the group. In our group, the general rule is that things told to either advisor in confidence can be shared with the other – unless we're explicitly asked not to.

54 - Taking care of yourself

You cannot take care of others unless you also take care of yourself.

Never let them tell you what to do

When I started out as an advisor I received an interesting piece of advice: never loan them money, and never let them tell you what to do.

I consider that some of the best advice I have ever received (the latter part in particular).

In a youth led group, part of what you are doing is defining areas where you will not, or cannot, tell the teens what to do (they are the ones making the decisions – so you can offer advice, but not directives).

But there is a difference between you not telling them what to do, and allowing them to tell you what to do. You should, at all times, reserve the right to determine your own actions. They can (and should) ask you to help out in different ways; and you can (and should) offer to help with various tasks as you feel appropriate. But the teens should never feel that they are in charge of your actions. You are the adult – the advisor. You are not a member of the group, and therefore are not subject to their direction.

Oh, and about loaning money? I have given teens money on occasion – say if they ran short on train fare, or for a phone call.[30] I've even treated for a meal. But I never expect money back on these occasions. I always encourage them to borrow from each other first.

---

[30] Remember, I started advising long before every kid had a cell phone.

Insist on being treated as a person

It is human nature to see people in terms of their roles: the faceless bureaucrat, the police officer, the teacher, the parent. I confess, I've sometimes yelled at a phone solicitor who had the nerve to interrupt my dinner, even though I know that person is just an ordinary individual trying to make a living.

There will be times you are seen as just "the advisor", "the teacher", or whatever title you happen to have. When you feel this is happening, don't be afraid to speak up. Be explicit and explain why you are feeling the way you are and how you expect to be treated. This is not just important for your sake. In a youth led group some of the teens will have titles as well, and will on occasion be treated by others based on that role or title. They need to see how to respond to this.

Here is an example:

There was a period where I had a co-advisor who... well, let's just say it was not my choice to work with him. His biggest problem was that while the teens liked him, they did not respect him. As such, many of them treated him very poorly, even making fun of him right to his face.

One day, I had a chance to ask the chapter president why they treated him that way, adding "you know, if you guys treated me that way, I'd walk in a minute."

He looked at me and answered: "Dan, we know that. That's why we don't treat you that way."

I'm not suggesting you threaten to resign on every personal slight. They are teenagers, and will (rightly) be far more concerned about themselves and their peers than about you. When you experience lack of consideration (which you will), you can gently but firmly remind them that you are deserving of consideration; this is one of the ways you'll teach them to consider not just you, but others.

But if you find yourself being treated as an object and taken completely for granted, call them on it. Definitely call in your supervisor to help you with this. And if they won't correct the situation, it may be time to walk and find a group that will be more appreciative of your efforts.[31]

By the way, the same applies to being treated with respect by your supervisor or management.

Dealing with mistakes

You are going to make mistakes. Some of those mistakes will hurt someone. You are going to have failures – teens who, through choice or circumstance, go the wrong way, and whom you are unable to help, or help enough. You are going to miss things – opportunities where you might have made a difference, but now it's too late.

When these things happen, you are going to feel terrible. No apology will be enough. You will probably feel inadequate and full of self-doubt. You may feel a failure. You will second-guess your decisions. You will wonder if it's worth it.

If you're good (and if you feel this way when you make mistakes, I assure you that you're one of the good ones), your only consolation will be this: even though you make mistakes, you are doing more good than harm.

I realize that may seem like scant consolation. But after twenty years, working with hundreds of teens, and having

[31] There are many different kinds of organizations. Some work with teens who have issues such that you will be expected to deal with more disrespect than others. If this is your job, walking may not be an option. The principle applies even if in practice you may not be able to achieve the kind of treatment that you deserve.

made my share of mistakes – it's the best I can offer. Try not to be too hard on yourself, and remember your successes. They'll get you through the tough times.

Joy and frustration

There's an odd dichotomy of working with teens (and kids in general).

On one hand, sometimes what you do and say matters. Even an innocent phrase can have a huge impact, and you may not even know it happened (now there's a scary thought).

On the other hand, frequently what you do and say will make little or no difference. Sometimes, despite your best efforts, the teens will make poor decisions – and nothing you can do will change that. You can spend hours to plan the most creative workshop, and nobody will seemingly learn a thing. The truth is, you can't "fix" people – nor help those who do not want help.

This is a dichotomy that every teacher knows, that every youth advisor struggles with, and that drives many parents crazy.

I would not presume to have the answers on how to deal with this dilemma – but I can offer a few thoughts that might help.

- Do not take credit for their success. Even if you did contribute to that success, it is their success (as it would not have been possible without their actions and choices).
- Do not take the blame for their failures. Their choices are far more important than anything you can do. Parents often ask themselves, "Where did we go wrong?" Sometimes it's the parents fault, but often it

is not. Whose fault it is ultimately doesn't change the facts, nor does looking back substitute for good choices going forward.

- Everyone has different strengths and weaknesses. So does every community. The approaches and techniques I describe here will not turn every teen into a great leader, nor every group into a model youth-led community. Look for progress, improvement, and the small victories. Take joy in those small victories, and try not to let the failures frustrate you too much.

- You will see miracles, sometimes when you least expect them. You will see courage to match that of any hero, kindness that may bring you to tears, and leadership to match the greatest of presidents. Remember these moments.

Burnout

Burnout is a common affliction among those who work with kids and teens (teachers in particular). I am often asked how I've managed to avoid it after all these years.

The answer is: I haven't. But I have been able to manage it.

Focusing on developing leadership among the teens you work with is, surprisingly enough, a great way to minimize the chance of burnout. Why? Because a key part of youth leadership is getting the teens to actually do the work. They can do much more than decide what events to hold – they can research the event, make calls, place reservations, and basically handle every aspect of the event. And everything they do is something you don't have to do yourself.

In fact, you don't even need to pay attention to every aspect of the event – remember, part of teaching leadership is allowing them to make mistakes. So all you need to do is go over the critical issues and offer advice when asked. That's considerably less work than doing everything yourself.

The same applies to the events themselves. If the teens are taking responsibility for running the show (and cleaning up afterwards), you don't have to do more than keep an eye on things. And if they know to call you when problems occur, you can even take a nap during the event.

The more the teens can do, the less you need to do. The less you need to do, the longer you can go without getting burned out.

Aside from that, you can avoid burnout by pacing yourself. While I have been a youth group advisor for over 20 years, my level of engagement has varied considerably in that time based on my own energy and the needs of the group. A few weeks of downtime now and again are essential.

That's all well and good for part time volunteers, but what about those of you whose livelihood is at stake? Especially those of you who are expected to put in a substantial amount of unpaid overtime. Or those of you who put in extra time because it is so desperately needed. You'll need to be much more proactive in taking care of yourself. There are numerous online resources available to help you, and your organization may also provide counseling and resources.

Some of the techniques you can learn include:

- How to identify where the greatest pressure or stress is coming from.
- How to be assertive in the ways you can control or influence your workload.
- How to deal with the people and political issues in your organization (there are always political issues).

- Practice relaxation techniques. Exercise regularly to promote health and prevent exhaustion.
- Remember to spend enough time on the fun and rewarding parts of your job. For example: be sure to spend some time with the teens you really like instead of spending all of your time dealing with troublemakers and those in need.

Carry an umbrella insurance policy

We live in a litigious society. That said, in more than 20 years as an advisor, not one of the many advisors I've worked with has had any legal trouble at all. Only twice in that time did I have to consult with an attorney, in both cases just to help me understand some issues (once having to do with personal liability, the other a question of trademark use).

Most youth organizations have insurance policies that provide some degree of coverage for staff and volunteers. Your supervisor should be able to give you more details on this. That said, you can purchase an excess liability policy (often called an umbrella policy) as a rider on your homeowners or renters insurance. This kind of insurance is surprisingly inexpensive, and can offer you additional peace of mind.

Tax deductions for volunteers

If you are a volunteer for a non-profit organization, many of the expenses that you have will be partially or fully tax deductible. You can read more in Publication 526 at http://irs.gov or talk to a friendly accountant.[32]

---

[32] This applies to U.S. readers. Contact your local tax agency for the rules that apply to you.

Part V - For Teachers and Parents

Being a youth group advisor is a unique position. You are not a teacher, but you teach. You are not a parent, yet you will find yourself "parenting" in some sense for some of the teens.

In a group where the youth have a strong leadership role, the position is even more unusual. It may be the only opportunity where an adult can be present and welcome on the teenagers' turf (schools generally belong to the teachers, home to the parents) – offering a unique opportunity to witness what it really is like to be a teen today.

Parents sometime half jokingly say that I know more about what their kids are up to than they do. I regret to say that this is often the case.

If an advisor can also be a teacher and parent, then certainly teachers and parents can pick up a trick or two from advisors. That is a part of what I'll share with you in this chapter. I will also discuss some of the issues that tend to come up between teens, teachers and parents, and how some of the concepts presented in this book can help resolve these issues.

55 - For Teachers

Here's a funny story. I've never been a full time classroom teacher; but I did teach evening religious school classes for many years. I was thrown into my first classroom with absolutely no training. Not having any idea how to teach in a classroom, I had to draw on the only relevant experience I did have – a few summers as a camp counselor. My classroom became an extension of summer camp – where I applied all of the different programming approaches you read about in Chapter 41. I would always request the classroom farthest away from the rest of the school – because my classes tended to be loud, with a lot of activity. Many of my classes involved splitting the class into groups and putting students in charge of leading discussions, putting on skits, or preparing presentations. When I knew I was going to be absent, I would even prepare lesson packets so student leaders could run the class when I was away.

In effect, without realizing it, my classes had become defacto youth groups and I was just naturally incorporating leadership training.

Then, at the end of one term over twenty years ago, a group of students in one of my more successful classes drafted me to become the advisor for their actual youth group – which started the chain of events that ultimately resulted in this book.

Respect

It would be politically correct at this point for me to say a bunch of nice things about teachers – the hard work you put in, the inadequate resources you are given, the challenging rules, regulations and administration you have to deal with. I could go on and on. And you know what? There are many teachers for whom all of that is true. I hear about them from the teens.

I hear about the other teachers too. You know what the biggest complaint I hear is? It's not poor teaching. It's disrespect. Teachers who publicly humiliate students. Teachers who don't listen to legitimate complaints. Teachers who would rather teach a falsehood than admit they do not know everything.

Do you remember one of the very first guiding principles in this book? Don't try to get them to like you; earn their respect. This principle applies to teachers as well. You might say that teachers deserve respect and shouldn't need to earn it. That's a legitimate argument, but I humbly suggest that it doesn't matter if you deserve respect because of your role – you should earn it anyway.

Leadership in the classroom

You know the documentaries and movies that show teachers whose classrooms are flurries of creative lesson plans, with highly engaged and motivated students who work together in groups and take initiative to not just learn the assigned material, but go beyond it?

I know these classrooms exist, and I recall a handful of moments like that in my own time as a student that captured some of that magic – but honestly, they were few and far between. The teachers in those documentaries make it look easy, and it isn't.

Youth group advisors have a number of advantages and disadvantages over classroom teachers when it comes to developing leadership. On the advantage side, the teens are usually there because they want to be there. As you may have noticed, not every teen is quite so fond of school. It's a lot easier to be motivated to engage in something you are not being forced to attend. A youth group advisor generally has more freedom to delegate authority to the teens – there are more decisions they can make. A classroom teacher is limited not just by school rules and policies, but by the requirement to teach a particular curriculum and strive to get students to achieve high test scores.

Teachers do have the advantage, however, of actually having real authority to teach. If a teacher wants students to practice speaking in front of the class, he or she simply requires that as part of the grade. This may not always be as effective as when a student asks to learn a skill, but that doesn't mean it lacks all benefit.

As a teacher you can seek out classroom techniques that require students to develop leadership skills. All of the program types described in Part III of this book on "Programs and activities" can be adapted for classroom use, and most can be adapted to almost any subject. Even occasional use of leadership oriented programming can have an impact.

Guiding principles

Most of the guiding principles in Part I of this book are relevant to classroom teachers. The following is a quick review of these principles, along with comments on their applicability.

- **Anything they can do, they should do** – This one has limited applicability in the classroom, but can be applied to specific scenarios such as assignments or projects.

- **Don't try to get them to like you; earn their respect** – Absolutely true, as any veteran teacher knows.
- **Thou shalt not lie** – Sincerity counts in the classroom as well.
- **Let them fail** – In school, this is not so much a guideline as an inevitability. Teachers rarely have the time or resources to prevent failure. Still, some give up way too soon.
- **Limits** – Sound policy in any classroom.
- **Find ways to say yes** – You'll be amazed how effective this can be.
- **Initiative and control** – This is one of the few guidelines that just does not apply to school. While you can and should create opportunities for teens to take initiative, you must keep control over your classroom.
- **Admit your hypocrisies** – Most students will find this a breath of fresh air. And if you are confident, it will always strengthen your position.
- **Role modeling is everything** – Role modeling is everything. Really.
- **Apologize for your mistakes** – You want them to admit their mistakes? Set the example.
- **Set high expectations, but not perfection** – Every good teacher knows this one.
- **You really don't know best** – Hard to admit, but true at school as well.
- **Wait – most problems solve themselves** – Unfortunately, you will rarely have enough classroom hours to be able to follow this guideline.

- **Be a back-seat driver** – Not at school. As teacher, you are always the main leader in your classroom. This is why being a good role model is particularly important. What you can't give them in the form of actual leadership, you can compensate for by demonstrating excellent leadership in your role as a teacher.

- **Don't take it personally** – Youth group advisors have a much easier time stepping out of the "advisor" title and insisting on being treated as a person. As a teacher, you will tend to be seen as a teacher always. Your students have spent too many years being conditioned to seeing the teacher as the role and not the person. You will not overcome this easily. One of the best ways to be seen as a person is to work with the teens outside of the classroom – perhaps, as a club advisor.

  Because you will tend to be seen as a "teacher" rather than a person, there will be a tendency for teens to be less than considerate in the things they say about you (behind your back and in person). They will also react to the position – not knowing the person holding it.

  So when they disobey or you find out what they are saying about you, try not to take it personally. If you are able to earn their respect, these kinds of problems will become rare.

- **Talking back is good** – Some teachers have a very hard time with students who argue with them. Admittedly, many students don't know how to argue their points in a calm, reasoned and respectful manner. Instead of shutting down the argument, try showing them how to do so properly. Give them guidance on how they can disagree with you and get you to listen; and when they do, be sure to listen carefully. And if you still disagree, explain your reasoning.

- **Plant seeds** – Good teachers do this instinctively.
- **Boundaries and rules** - This one is not very applicable, in that the boundaries and rules for teachers are fairly clear-cut and explicit.
- **Being there** – It's your job. You're going to be there whether you like it or not. Try to like it though. A good attitude when things are tough also sets a good example.
- **Consistency** – Definitely good for teachers.
- **Who owns the group?** – You own the group. But if you can give students a sense of ownership over the class, it can have an amazing positive impact on every aspect of the classroom experience (for you and your students).
- **Trust** – Important in the classroom as well.
- **Remember the carrot** – Good teachers are very good at this.
- **Turf and communication** – Not applicable for schools. Your classroom is your turf.

The techniques described in Part II can also be applied and taught in school with only minor changes.

56 - For Parents

I have so much respect for parents.

Let's face it, compared to being a parent, being a youth group advisor is easy – after a few hours, the kids go home. We get them in small doses. We don't have to show up for every event. But parents are always on duty in one way or another.

For many years, I felt it was presumptuous for me to offer advice to parents; and was somewhat surprised when parents would approach me for advice. But I've come to see otherwise. You see, while an experienced youth group advisor can't possibly know your kid as well as you do, they (like teachers) have seen a lot of kids grow up. They may not have the depth of experience with your child, but they have a breadth of experience that is unmatched. Moreover, unlike teachers, they often know the teens on their own turf – not just in the limited classroom setting.

Or put another way: a teacher knows what teens are like in class and maybe an occasional field trip. I know what they are like at weekend conventions, at dances, on trips, while playing sports, while just hanging out, while getting along well, while facing conflict, and pretty much any other situation you can imagine.

And when it comes to teens dealing with parents, I've gotten an earful.

Why teens talk to advisors

Parents sometimes have a difficult time with the fact that their son or daughter will talk to their youth group advisor about issues that they won't discuss with them. It is important to take a few moments and understand why that is – it goes to the heart of the relationship between parents and their teens.

Somewhere during the teen years is when teenagers begin to see you as a person and not just Mom or Dad. But even when this happens, you are always their parent. These days, most adults that teens deal with are either parents, family members, teachers, coaches or bosses – people in positions of authority who spend a lot of their time telling teens what to do.

For some teens, their youth group advisor may be one of the first adults they meet with whom they can have a conversation as equals, and who treats them as an adult (or as they believe an adult would be treated).

Recently I did a presentation to a group consisting of chapter members and their parents. Afterwards, one of the older members came up to me somewhat in shock. What surprised him was his realization that I spoke to the parents exactly the same way I spoke to the teens. Of course, the reality is that I generally speak to the teens the same way I would speak with adults – with respect, and as equals.

As a parent, you're always a parent – and that's how it should be. But this fundamental difference is one of the reasons that teens will inevitably communicate differently with advisors than parents.

Another common theme is fear. Teens are sometimes afraid to talk to their parents because they are afraid of the response, whether it is anger or, more often, disappointment. This frequently applies to advisors as well, but usually not to the same degree. Sometimes teens will try things out on advisors to see how they respond, before bringing the issue up with their parents (because it is less risky). Advisors are much less likely to overreact because, frankly, we don't care as much as parents do (and that's how it should be – if the advisor cares about a teen more than a parent does, there's a problem somewhere).

Communication breakdown

As an advisor, I love it when teens have good relations with their parents. For one thing, I've found that the strongest and most successful teen leaders always have the best parental support. And those teens who are able to talk to their parents about issues don't need me as much, freeing my time to help others, to focus on teaching skills, or to take a nice long nap.

When teens complain about their parents, there are usually communication problems. Sometimes teens are afraid to talk to their parents. Sometimes they are frustrated because every time they try their parents are too busy or don't really listen or every attempt results in an argument. In these cases, I try to help the teen figure out ways to change their approach (since families often have the same argument over and over, each person sticking with their routine and comfortable role). For example: I might encourage them to write a note or send an email, or to try active listening techniques.

The one thing I never do is act as an intermediary between parents and their teens. An intermediary should be someone objective who can help two parties communicate, but does not take sides. As a youth group advisor, I am always on the teen's side – an advocate, not an arbitrator.

There are plenty of resources and books for parents on raising and communicating with teenagers, I won't try to recreate them here. I'll just note a few points:

- When communication breaks down between you and your teens, you may blame them, and they may blame you. Figuring out who is at fault isn't particularly productive. Keep making the effort to communicate, and try different approaches.
- It's easier to talk to teens than to listen to them. But listening is more important.
- The techniques described in this book can help. Note especially the communication techniques in Part II, and Chapter 24 on "Turf and communication".
- Change the venue. Go on a road trip. Take a cruise. Take a hike in the woods. Have a midnight snack. Let your teen take you somewhere they like.
- When your teen finally starts talking, embrace the moment. Stay up all night if that is what it takes, even if it means missing school or work the next day. If you really want open communication, it will more often be on their schedule than yours.

Separation and independence

I have yet to meet a teen who does not, at some time or another, have a conflict with his or her parents. "They don't trust me" and, "They don't understand me" are common refrains. But ultimately it comes down to the problem of dealing with change.

At 12 you have a child who is generally dependent and more or less obedient. By 18 that person has grown into an adult, who is legally independent and can typically be asked but not commanded. That's six years to go from dependence to independence. Herein lies the problem:

- The rate at which a teen is ready for independence varies during that time, and varies based on the subject at hand.
- Your opinion of what your teen is ready for may not match his or her view.
- In the ideal world, you would give your teen exactly the amount of independence that they are actually ready to handle, and that amount would be just a bit more than they themselves believe they are ready for. But the chances that you or your teen will have perfect judgment on this matter are vanishingly small.

Conflicts relating to independence are inevitable. But if you can keep open communication channels, you should be able resolve issues as they arise without too much difficulty. Just remember that it will require negotiation and compromise on both sides.

Keep your eyes open for real problems

It's tough to be a teenager today. It's a cliché, but it's true nonetheless. It is important that you remain engaged. To this day I am astonished by the number of parents who see our youth group as a baby-sitting service, barely aware of what goes on within the group, and oblivious to what their teens are doing outside of the group.

One tip I hear a lot is to watch for changes in behavior, friends, or grades – and that these can be a sign of problems such as drug use. While true in some cases, this tip is a bit simplistic. Changes in behavior, friends, or grades is actually very common in the teen years, and aren't necessarily cause for concern. What's more, some teens can use drugs recreationally without any significant impact on their lives – you wouldn't know they were doing it if they didn't tell you. Here are some additional, still somewhat simplistic, but hopefully useful tips.

- A change in friends is not necessarily a problem. But a change to friends who you don't like, is another matter (unless, of course, you don't like any teens – in which case your judgment won't mean much).
- While it's true that some teens try drugs and alcohol for fun, and some due to peer pressure, some use them as a form of self-medication when they are suffering from depression. Teen depression is a real problem; if you suspect it, don't wait to seek out professional help and advice. Remember, teenagers' brains are changing as quickly as their bodies – and it's not at all unusual for there to be some problems adjusting. Drug use may be the symptom of an underlying problem, not the cause.

Guiding principles

Most of the guiding principles in Part I of this book are relevant to parents. The following is a quick review of these principles, along with comments on their applicability.

- **Anything they can do, they should do** – This is not nearly as strong a guideline at home as it is in a youth group. You are a family, after all, and should be doing things for each other and to support each other. But make it a two way street – be sure there are times where you don't step in and do things for them, and times where you expect them to do things for you or for the family.

- **Don't try to get them to like you; earn their respect** – Your teenager knows you better than almost anyone, and knows exactly how to push your buttons. And your relationship will run the gamut from love to hate to admiration to disdain, often in the span of hours. So saying you should earn your teens respect seems rather trite. Perhaps it is better to say you should strive to be worthy of respect.

- **Thou shalt not lie** – Honesty is important at home as well.

- **Let them fail** – Letting your kids make mistakes and learn from them is another great gift you can give them. Offer advice, but sometimes give them permission to ignore it and do what they think is best. Be there to help pick them up afterwards.

- **Limits** – Most teens really do want limits. They want clear and consistent limits that make sense. They want the ability to negotiate those limits that they feel are unreasonable. Beyond that, strive to give them as much freedom and independence as you can, as long as they stay within those limits – it's in that freedom that they will gain confidence and build self-esteem.

- **Find ways to say yes** – How many times a day do you say no? When you say yes, is it with a reluctant "I'll think about it" or "maybe"? Try turning things around. See what happens if you are reluctant and apologetic (but firm) when you say no. But respond with a positive and enthusiastic YES! the rest of the time. It may surprise your teen out at first, but I think you'll like the results.

- **Initiative and control** – Try to find ways to encourage initiative and grant control to your teen.
- **Admit your hypocrisies** – Your teens already know your limitations and failings. You might as well admit them.
- **Role modeling is everything** – You are your kids' greatest role model. They learn far more from what you do than from what you say.
- **Apologize for your mistakes** – You want them to admit their mistakes? Set the example.
- **Set high expectations, but not perfection** – High expectations are good, but be patient. Your teen's schedule may not match yours. If it's not urgent, give them time to meet those expectations.
- **You really don't know best** – You may think you know your teen better than they know themselves. But you probably don't. First, they are changing very quickly – so chances are whatever you think you know about them is already obsolete. Second, they are growing up in a world that is already radically different from the one you grew up in. So even if you think you know best, why not take the time to ask them what they think and discuss it before making a decision? You may be surprised by what you learn.
- **Wait – most problems solve themselves** – This is true. But don't be afraid to step in if the problem is serious and you aren't seeing improvement.
- **Be a back-seat driver** – This one isn't really applicable – at least not directly. But remember – no matter how much you love them, it is ultimately their life. Your job is to put them in the driver's seat.

- **Don't take it personally** – This principle works well for advisors and teachers, but not parents. You should take things personally – you're their parent. That said, the responses discussed in this section – to respond thoughtfully to incidents and seek out consequences that have a positive impact, are absolutely relevant to parents as well.

- **Talking back is good** – Your teenager is going to talk back to you (if he or she never talks back, you may have a greater problem). Since you have to deal with it anyway, teach them to do so properly. If you have a teen who confronts you calmly and rationally, you will have a teen who will be able to use those skills throughout their life with managers or employees. How do you teach this? Both by telling them how you expect to be treated and by making sure that they are often successful in their negotiation when they approach you in that manner (and always fail when they are angry and disrespectful).

- **Plant seeds** – Parents can't help but plant seeds. Try to make them good ones.

- **Boundaries and rules** - This one is not very clear-cut when it comes to parents. Some parents are parents 24/7. Others are also friends. The balance varies by individual and there is no clear right approach.

- **Being there** – This is very important. Note especially the comments about quality time.

- **Consistency** – Definitely good for parents.

- **Who owns the group?** – In this context, the group is your family. And while parents are the head of the family (or should be), if you can put your teen in charge of some aspects of family life on occasion, it can be a valuable experience.

- **Trust** – This is absolutely applicable to parents.
- **Remember the carrot** – You used to compliment your children when they were little. Have you stopped now that they are teens? If so, it's time to start again.
- **Turf and communication** – While the turf issue is not relevant to families, the communication issue is. Learn to text, email, chat, instant message or join whatever social network your teen is on. Don't impose or try to take over, but don't hesitate to use those communication channels. They can be far more effective then direct conversation – especially if you've been having communication issues.

Most of the techniques in Part II of this book can not only be used by parents effectively, they can dramatically improve your ability to engage and communicate with your teen. Try them all.

57 - For Teens

Hey! What do you think you're doing reading this book! It's clearly marked for advisors, teachers and parents – put it down right now!

Just kidding...

You are very welcome to read this book. Everything in it applies to you in one way or another. Aside from the leadership skills and techniques, I think it is important for teen leaders to understand the perspective of the advisors and staff - if only because the better you understand our perspective, the better you'll be able to assert yourself and stand up for what you want (which is a good thing).

If you'll allow me one bit of somewhat self-serving (but still sincere) advice: if you like what you've read here, go ahead and tell your advisors, teachers and parents to buy a copy. Or buy a copy for them. If you present it with a smile, they'll hopefully take no offense. After they've read it, talk it over with them. Just discussing the issues and techniques brought up here may go a long way to helping you work together.

Final Words

I never set out to be a youth group advisor. A few summers as a camp counselor, a bit of part time teaching, and some retreat weekends made for a fun type of community service activity to balance out an increasingly busy career as an engineer, software developer, entrepreneur and author.

More than twenty years ago, when a group of teens drafted me into staffing some events, it was more a matter of not wanting to turn them down than any desire to become their advisor. But then I realized that if I was going to staff events, I should do it properly and I became their advisor. A bit over 19 years ago, when that group had grown too large, they started a new chapter, which I joined as its first advisor. I told myself that the day would come when I'd get too old – unable to relate to the younger members just joining, and it would be time to quit. But somehow that didn't happen, and I stayed on.

I've always felt (and taught) that it's important to contribute to the community. And even though I tried some other things along the way, it is abundantly clear that nothing I've done has had the impact of being an advisor for that group.

They say that the best way to learn something is to teach it, and it's true. I've learned more at this job than I could have ever imagined. Knowing that I was a role model helped me to be a better person. It can't be a coincidence that soon after becoming an advisor for a group that emphasized leadership, I started putting those skills to use in my own life: starting a business, becoming an author, traveling and more. My life story changed from a boring tale of a 9-to-5 cubical wage slave, to a grand adventure beyond anything I had realistically dreamed.

I was fortunate. The summer camp I worked at so many years ago was not wealthy; so they relied heavily on counselors, and trained us well. Others: supervisors, directors and principals taught me – as did the alumni, other advisors and the teens themselves. And with time I've become (with all due modesty) a pretty good advisor. It even occasionally became my turn to be the teacher, helping to train other advisors.

But I'm not just a veteran advisor; I'm an author as well. And that means I presumably have the ability, and definitely have the responsibility, to share what I've learned with a larger circle than the other youth advisors in my little corner of the world. Which brings us to this book.

I'll be honest, it took a while to get around to finishing it. It's not like I expect to make any real money at it. I don't think there are that many advisors. And while I do believe any teacher or parent can benefit from this book, it's hard to say how many will ever find out about it. It's not as if it will be in Oprah's book club, you know?[33]

But however many copies it does end up selling, I'm glad I wrote it. Because I truly believe that the principles and techniques I've shared can help any advisor to be great. Great in the sense of having the power not so much to change teens' lives, but to help them to change each other's lives in amazing ways. And I believe these principles can also be helpful to

---

[33] That said, if you happen to know Oprah, or any other media person who talks about books, please let them know about it, and let me know so I can send them a review copy. I mean, you never know, right?

teachers and parents – offering them a new way and new techniques to make their challenging jobs just a bit easier.

For more than twenty years, I have watched uncertain, unskilled 13-year-olds enter our group, and in just a few years gain leadership skills beyond those of most adults. I have seen 16 and 17-year-olds who at 13 could barely stand in front of a room, give speeches before two hundred other teens with skills that would rival any world leader. I have seen kids who had no lives beyond homework and video games, plan complex events, trips, and weekend retreats, and take those skills on to college where they have become leaders at their school or fraternities, or founded their own organizations. And when they come back to visit (as almost all of them do), and they share stories about their accomplishments, they always express surprise at how impressed people are with their ability. "It's not such a big deal," they say. "It's the same kind of thing I was doing in our group while I was in high school."

But it is a big deal.

And while I and my co-advisors deserve but a small portion of the credit for what the teens have done for themselves, we know that we do matter – and that this work is worthwhile.

Appendix A – Drivers Handout

Congratulations. You have your license. You've finally convinced your parents to let you drive at events. Please take a few minutes to read this (I promise, it will prove worth your while).

First, the obvious

Look, you don't need me to tell you what an enormous responsibility it is to drive. You've heard that lecture from your driving teachers and from your parents. Every teen who drives knows how important it is to drive safely. You and I both know that there is little if anything that I can say that will make you choose to be one of the safe and careful drivers instead of one of the maniacs. But bear with me - there are a couple of things I must say:

Teens have died at events due to poor, careless and irresponsible drivers. I'm sure you'll agree that it is not nice to kill your fellow group members. It is also nice when prospective members survive long enough to at least join. 'nuff said.

OK, true enough, this doesn't happen often. But I'll tell you what does happen to the majority of teen drivers. They get careless, or show off, and one or more of the following happens:

- They get grounded by their parents (which does not help the perpetually driver hungry group one bit).
- They show off in a parking lot while parents are watching (which tends to discourage parents from letting their teens go to events or even join).
- They lose the use of their car, have to pay even higher insurance rates, and so on.

It may seem cool to do something crazy in a car, and I know it's hard to resist. But it's just not worth it.

OK - that's it for the safe driving speech. Now to the core of the survival guide (the things you may not already know).

Your rights as a driver

People spend so much time lecturing about the responsibilities of drivers, that they sometimes fail to discuss the responsibilities of passengers and the rights of drivers - so let's cover this very important subject first.

You have the right to do what is necessary to ensure the safety of your passengers and yourself

If a passenger is doing something that is in your judgment unsafe (for example: kicking the driver seat, wrestling, being so loud that it is distracting you), you have the right to pull over and stop until the situation is resolved. In an extreme case you can handle it as an emergency (as described later in this handout).

Now, this is a very powerful and important statement. It means that your passengers have a responsibility to behave and follow your directions with regards to safety issues. Safety is a very broad subject - anything that distracts you or upsets you as driver can be a safety issue (music too loud or music you hate, feet on ceilings, yelling, etc.) As driver, it is up to you to use your best judgment on this matter – not to use it as a power trip or otherwise take advantage of it.

You have the right to limit the number of passengers you carry

Some people are willing to fill every seat in their car, others are not. You should not take more people than you have seatbelts. If your parents have set a limit to the number of people you can carry, you have the right (and the responsibility) to refuse to take more no matter how much others beg. If your parents insist you follow other driving restrictions, you should do so.

Your rights and responsibilities as a passenger

You have the right to ride with a driver who you trust.

If you feel a driver is dangerous, do not enter their car – let the group leader or staff know. We will, if necessary, hold up the entire event until there are sufficient safe drivers to get us where we need to go.

You have a responsibility to follow all safety instructions from the driver.

Your responsibilities as a driver

It's really quite simple:

You have the RESPONSIBILITY to do what is necessary to ensure the safety of your passengers and yourself.

This means everything from driving safely to keeping your passengers in line. Let's get into some specifics.

- **Drive Safely.** (Elaboration: Driving when someone is sitting on or standing in front of or very close to your car is, by definition, unsafe – no exceptions).
- **Don't drive if you've recently taken any substance that can impair your driving.** This includes drugs or alcohol, and also any legal medication that is labeled with a warning not to drive.

- **Seat Belts**. You are responsible for making sure your passengers wear them.
- **If you bring people somewhere, don't leave until you know that they have a ride back.** That means, please don't leave an event without checking first that members will not be stranded. Hint: the easy way to fulfill this responsibility is to check out the ride status with the group leader or advisor – since this is also part of our job.
- **Don't let your passengers distract you or goad you into doing something unsafe**. (See the section on driver's rights)
- **Listen to your passengers**. Keeping them safe means more than driving safely. It means helping them if they are feeling ill or carsick. It means lending them a phone if they need to call home to avoid getting into trouble. SPECIAL NOTE: If a passenger feels you are driving unsafely, you probably are. Even if you are not being unsafe, slow down and be even more careful. Deal with the issue with them later (bring in your advisor if necessary). The freeway is no place for an argument.
- **See your passengers to their final destination**. This is one case where sometimes you should NOT listen to your passengers. It's your job to drop off your passengers at home or at the home of another member. You should NOT drop them off at a place that is closed or may be unsafe. Don't leave them behind somewhere even if they insist. Use your judgment – if a 17-year-old asks to be dropped off somewhere, go ahead unless it's obviously stupid or unsafe. If a

13-year-old asks to be dropped off somewhere, turn them down flat unless it's obviously safe and reasonable (your judgment is better than theirs).

Crisis situations (breakdowns, passengers, accidents and other emergencies)

First and most important – Don't Panic. As before, your primary responsibility is safety.

- **Handle any immediate safety issues first**. Do you need to pull off the road? Do you need to call for help? Do you need to apply first aid?
- **Handle any immediate legal issues next**. Do you need to exchange insurance or identification information? Do you need to call the police?
- **Figure out how to handle the situation**. GET ADVICE. If any staff or advisor is present, by now they should know what is going on and be helping you deal with the crisis. If not, there are a number of people who you can and should call for advice (not necessarily in this order): Your advisor, your parents, the parents of anyone else in your car, your organization's regional director (their number should be listed), any other parent or staff who you know.
- **Let people know about your change in plans**. If a breakdown or crisis situation is going to affect your arrival at your end destination, there are several things you should do: Call your final destination to let them know of your status. Call the parents of the passengers of the car to let them know as well. Call the staff or group leader to update them.

- **Do NOT accept rides from strangers**: No matter how nice they are (this applies to adult drivers as well).

Acknowledgements and Dedication

How can I even begin to acknowledge all of those who have taught me over the years? After all, they are the true contributors to this book.

It is my hope then, that they will see the book itself as my way of thanking them – knowing the lessons they taught will continue to spread and help teens everywhere. And while I can't list everyone, there are a few individuals who stand out, not because they are better or more important than others, but because they are representative of a time and place and set of lessons learned.

First my mom, Alicia Appleman-Jurman, author of "Alicia, My Story", who has taught more people through her story than I will ever reach. And to my dad, who had an amazing knack for getting along with all kinds of people.

To Normal Fassler-Katz and Emily Feigenson – The camp director and program director of the long closed Camp Komaroff, whose high expectations and outstanding training of ordinary camp counselors laid the foundation of everything that followed.

To Dottie Miller – my religious school principal who gave me free reign and gentle guidance in equal measure.

To Jason Doppelt, Justin Newman and Joel Papo, who along with their friends, recruited me to be an advisor.

To Debbie Findling – who was the regional director when I first became an advisor, and who set (or reset) me on the right path to learning how to teach teens to become leaders.

To Al Friedman – who taught me to trust myself.

To Eyal Soha, Eshel Haritan and Jeremy Palgon – the best co-advisors I could ever have asked for.

To Gilad Landan – who took us to Japan and proved to me that I should never doubt what teens are capable of when they set their minds to it.

To Roi Bachmutsky, Tomer Kagan, and all of the members and alumni who planned that amazing advisor appreciation event.

To my pre-publication readers, in particular Jeremy Palgon (who also helped enormously with the editing of the book) and Elliott Capsuto. Thanks for your comments and suggestions.

And last – and first...

To the members and alumni of Ramon AZA #195 – there are simply no words to express my thanks. This book is dedicated to you.

Made in United States
Orlando, FL
01 June 2022

18368618R00127